Dear Tu[...]
may this s[...]
history show You the grace
of God at work!
Peace & every good!
André ofm
Josef ofs

THREE HEROES
OF ASSISI IN WORLD WAR II

Bishop Giuseppe Nicolini,
Colonel Valentin Müller,
Don Aldo Brunacci

Josef Raischl, OFS
& André Cirino, OFM

Three Heroes of Assisi in World War II
Bishop Giuseppe Nicolini, Colonel Valentin Müller,
Don Aldo Brunacci
Edited and Written by
Josef Raischl, OFS and André Cirino, OFM

For information regarding permission, write to:
Tau Publishing, LLC
Attention: Permissions Dept.
4727 North 12th Street
Phoenix, AZ 85014

ISBN 978-1-61956-230-1

Second Edition May 2014
10 9 8 7 6 5 4 3 2

Published and printed in the United States of America by Tau Publishing, LLC.

♻ Text printed on 30% post-consumer waste recycled paper.

For additional inspirational books visit us at TauPublishing.com

TauPublishing.com

Words of Inspiration

> *"No more war,*
> *war never again!"*

Address of Paul VI
to the United Nations General Assembly
October 1965

May this prayer be answered!

CONTENTS

PREFACE

Jean François Godet-Calogeras

There is no such thing as a just war. For centuries, people have tried to justify their violence. When needed, they would use God—whatever name they would give God—to bless their armies, weapons, and killings. Throughout history even Christians forgot—and still forget today—that Jesus taught and lived unconditional nonviolence. Violence and war never solved problems or conflicts. When they are over, beyond an illusion of peace, they always generate more violence and other wars. And more victims.

And World War II was no exception. It was a war that a series of circumstances had arguably made inevitable, but inevitability is not justice. Because of a few, tens of millions of men and women went through hell, and tens of millions of them never had the luck nor the grace to see the end of it. And those who did never forgot.

History books often attach glory to war. And glory there is, but the real one is not in winning battles, taking over strategic places, and overcoming enemies. The real glory is in the human actions of compassion, care and love at the risk of one's life. Those actions happen and should get more attention than the acts of violence. History ought to be told through the positive actions of the loving, the caring and the peacemaking.

A small city of central Italy has had such glory for centuries: Assisi, the city of Saint Francis, the thirteenth century man who spoke to the birds and tamed a wolf. If the popular image is not wrong, it should not hide the fact that Francis' life is filled with acts of compassion and peace: care for the poor and the outcast, reconciliation between a bishop and a mayor of the city, attempt at a nonviolent resolution of a crusade, outreach to those medieval Christianity considered as the worst enemies, the Muslims. All that because Francis, in his own words, wanted to live according to the Gospel and follow the teachings and the footsteps of Jesus Christ.

In 1943-1944, amidst the horrors of the most murderous conflict in human history, Assisi had another time of true glory. While the Allies had just landed in Sicily and with great difficulty were progressing north from southern Italy, Assisi was occupied by German troops. There, two men worked together to do something constructive rather than destructive: the Bishop of Assisi, Giuseppe Nicolini, and the German officer in command, a medical doctor from Bavaria, Colonel Valentin Müller. Divided by the war opposing their countries, the two men remained nevertheless united by their Christian faith and its mandate of unconditional love. They obtained that Assisi be made hospital city, a city for medical care, not for military confrontation; a city for healing, not for fighting.

A little later, another positive action was started, this time with the participation of a third local hero. Bishop Nicolini received a letter from the Secretariat of State of the Vatican urging him to provide aid for the growing number of Jewish refugees fleeing the Nazi persecution. The bishop asked his secretary to help him create and develop the underground network that would shelter and save, without the knowledge of the German occupants, more than two hundred Jews coming from various regions of Europe. The secretary was Don Aldo Brunacci, who was barely thirty years old at the time.

This book relates the story of what happened, thanks to those three men, and how, because they were human beings in distress, Jews were rescued by caring Christians that war had officially made enemies. Obviously, Colonel Müller was never informed or made an accomplice to the rescue of the Jews: it would have made him a traitor, and would have most certainly compromised the whole operation. Everything had to remain underground. But Colonel Müller's humanitarian acts and decisions did help, and one might think that, intelligent as he was, he had intuited what was going on in the Umbrian city in those days. His repeated interventions against ruthless SS and Gestapo members were certainly and clearly in favor of the oppressed.

Don Aldo Brunacci was the last survivor of that trio of beautiful heroes. And prefacing this book gives me an opportunity to celebrate the bond of friendship that had grown for more than thirty years, since those days of October 1974 when I first came to Assisi for a conference of the International Society of Franciscan Studies of which Don Aldo was an active member, being a recognized scholar himself. Many times Don Aldo had told the story of what happened in Assisi during World War II. And he was a lively, passionate story teller. But always did he praise the courageous action of Bishop Nicolini, Colonel Müller, and the good Assisian people who helped; always did he remember how those Jewish families became his friends. Very often—I witnessed it several times—Don Aldo would be asked the question: why? Why did you risk your life for some Jews, for some people who were not Christian? Don Aldo's answer was always the same, simple and clear, unpretentious and self-explanatory: Because that is what the Gospel asks a Christian to do. The unconditional mandate of love so well illustrated in the parable of the Good Samaritan.

What happened in Assisi now many years ago remains an inspiration for us today, in our not-so-peaceful world. What happened then shows what happens when human beings put their true and deep beliefs into practice, no matter what; when human beings put their faith and love above any other worldly loyalty. Obedience to God comes before obedience to people, the early disciples of Christ used to say. Bishop Nicolini, Colonel Müller, and Don Aldo Brunacci did not do anything less in the city of Saint Francis, the brother and the peacemaker. And it is for good reason that, as the authentic Assisian he was, Don Aldo liked to say, with a blend of humility and pride, that he was *un francescano di cuore*, a Franciscan at heart. Through his deeds, he certainly showed how truly he was.

Jean François Godet-Calogeras, Ph.D.
Professor of Franciscan Studies
Saint Bonaventure University

INTRODUCTION

Josef Raischl and André Cirino

War knows no beauty and recognizes no art. It is a question of life and death, of victory and defeat. Destruction and devastation are its inevitable consequences. Soldiers can only show mercy and compassion in thinking of their homeland. What good are guarantees? What is the use of neutral zones? Military advantage is the first rule of war in every age.

On 11 May 1944 the Benedictine Abbey of Montecassino shared in the destiny of destruction in war. Centuries of art and culture were reduced to dust in minutes. Assisi—that Umbrian town filled with historical art and monuments dear to the spirituality of millions of people—could have suffered a similar fate. Assisi's survival is no accident.

People look for things to do, and that includes good things as well. In the midst of every crisis and conflict there are stout-hearted people who are signs of hope in the midst of anguish and doubt. Individuals have put all kinds of plans into motion, have kept cool heads and used every bit of their creativity and determination without losing sight of values such as beauty, justice and unity.

That is what this book is meant to recall. Amidst all the

horrible things that happened, its purpose is to document the good things that happened. Unfortunately, that is not what happened in the case of the film by Dr. Alexander Ramati, *Assisi Underground* (1984).

In spite of the thoroughly researched and well-documented work of Francesco Santucci—*Assisi 1943-1944, Documenti Per Una Storia*—Assisi today, even with contributions from many eye-witnesses, cannot compete with the excitement

and popularity of a film. For this reason we have chosen to translate and publish these extracts in the hope that it may help us to focus on real persons and events. Doubtless, Francis of Assisi was one of those real persons, as was Clare. And many people

St. Clare, credited with saving Assisi in 1241 from invasion by the Saracens.

followed in their footsteps and discovered new ways of living their life according to the Gospel of Jesus.

Today, too, real people need our attention and solidarity. And we and our world need these real people, as real as the three heroes[1] described in this little book: Bishop Giuseppe Placido Nicolini, Bishop of Assisi until his death in 1973; Colonel Valentin Müller, MD Commander of the

---

1   We chose the word "hero" to describe these three protagonists not only because we see them as heroes, but also because some contributors to this book have actually called them heroes.

city of Assisi (†1951); Don[2] Aldo Brunacci (†2007), the last surviving witness. We are especially grateful for the gift of his life and for his simple yet powerful presence in Assisi.

Both of us travelled to Assisi in 1987 as part of a study week in conjunction with the Institute for Franciscan Spirituality at the *Antonianum* in Rome. We lodged just across the road from the Bishop's ancient palace at Santa Maria Maggiore. André already knew Don Aldo Brunacci by then, and Josef was poised to marry the granddaughter of Colonel Valentin Müller, Bernadette Müller. So both of us connected early on with the history of this holy place. Finally, in 1999, in order to report more accurately on the facts concerning Assisi during the war years 1943-44, we decided to translate a portion of Santucci's work. Josef was in close contact with his wife's family and André spent several months each year at Casa Papa Giovanni with Don Aldo Brunacci. So the book grew out of this backdrop.

We are aware of many repetitions in the accounts of these historical events, and we decided not to edit them out so that the story becomes more familiar to us, even part of us. In the accounts we have chosen, some facts, at times very minor, may vary such as the number of Jewish people saved. This latter fact remains inaccurate because, as Don Aldo told us, records of names were not kept so as to protect the absorption of the Jews into the city population and "prudence dictated that nothing should be written down."[3]

---

2   In Italian, secular (diocesan) priests are given the title "Don," while religious priests are called "Padre."

3   See p. 70.

We would like to thank all those people who helped make this book possible and encouraged us, especially all who graciously gave us reprint permissions for material chosen for this book. We express our gratitude to Professor Francesco Santucci, the author of the basic historical work, who agreed to the translation of some excerpts. We are grateful to Sister Nancy Celaschi, a Franciscan from the USA, who translated many texts originally in Italian. We would also like to thank Dr. Valentin Müller's family, especially his two children, Dr. Irmgard Heinemann (†2009) and Dr. Robert Müller (†2005) for their recollections. We thank Jona Raischl for use of his photographs. Our gratitude to Professor Jean-François Godet-Calogeras for graciously contributing the preface to this work. Finally, our deep appreciation extends to Don Aldo Brunacci. He not only wrote about this time in history, but was intimately involved as an actor in these historical events. We hope that we have fulfilled his desire to "publish all the documents in my possession regarding the events in question.... I hope to do this as soon as possible, because only the truth deserves to be known."[4]

Dachau/New York, 2013
Josef Raischl, OFS and André Cirino, OFM

---

4   See p. 136. Don Aldo Brunacci was still alive for the publication of the first edition of this work in 2005.

CHRONOLOGY 1943-44

Historical overview[1]

1943

25 July	Fascism was overthrown in Italy. Mussolini is captured.
September	British and American troops landed in southern Italy. German and Italian troops fought the Allies and the Italian Resistance.
9 September	The Germans occupied Assisi.
Mid-September	Benito Mussolini was freed by the Germans and proclaims the Repubblica Sociale Italiana.
16 October	The Germans began their purge of the Jewish ghetto in Rome.
30 October	Allied planes bombed the Sant' Egidio Airport near Assisi.

1   Santucci, pp. 299-304. Used with permission.

1944

7 January	Seventeen Assisians died in the bombardment of Sant'Egidio.
1 March	Dr. Müller was named commander of the German troops in Assisi.
11 May	The Abbey of Montecassino was bombed and completely destroyed.
31 May	General Kesselring, Supreme Commander of German troops in Italy, agreed to declare Assisi a hospital city.
4 June	Rome was liberated by the Allied troops.
16 June	German troops, together with the wounded, left Assisi.
17 June	The Allies established a new municipal government in Assisi.
31 August	By agreement of the Vatican, the Bishop of Assisi and the army command, Assisi was to be kept free of troops and military exercises.

SAVING ASSISI DURING WORLD WAR II

Francesco Santucci

THE GERMAN OCCUPATION OF ASSISI [1]
8 September 1943—16 June 1944

THE ARRIVAL OF THE FIRST GERMAN DIVISIONS

After 8 September 1943 the first Germans arrived in Assisi, "driving the rich people out of the Subasio, Giotto and Savoia Hotels."[2] Only a few days before the ceasefire an Italian-German meeting was held in the holy city. Officially it was about economic matters, but in reality it dealt with military questions. The meeting was held in the Hotel Subasio. At that time there were rumors of greater military developments in Assisi. On 8 September a German captain on an exploration trip entered the courtyard of the Sacro Convento in a truck, carrying a hand grenade and automatic weapon to subject the Custos "to a relentless interrogation on various topics."[3]

During the first few days of October 1943 the Germans

---

1   Santucci, pp. 35-51, *Occupazione tedesca della città*. Used with permission. English translation by Nancy Celaschi, OSF.

2   Cf. B. Mansi, *Relazione circa alcune particolari attività dei Frati Minori Conventuali di Assisi durante la presente guerra*, 12 August 1944, Archives of the Sacro Convento, b. *Santa Sede—Telegrammi, Rescritti, Decreti*, typewritten manuscript, p. 9.

3   Ibid., p. 10.

occupied the city with some troops from the airborne forces and military medical corps. The former, who worked at the nearby Sant'Egidio airfield, were lodged at the Subasio Hotel; the latter were billeted at the former Italian convalescent home (today the Seraphic Institute) to establish the first German field hospital (*Feld Lazarett*) in Assisi.[4]

After 8 September 1943 the Locatelli Palace[5] was designated to house the German military wounded. It served in this capacity until 16 June 1944. (Beginning on 17 June 1944 it would house Allied soldiers and partisan formations)[6].

A second hospital was established several days later in the buildings of the Prince of Naples National Home for Orphans of Teachers:

> On 10 October, with absolutely no warning, German forces occupied the whole complex, except for the palazzina…and the 29 orphans were left to live and study in those few rooms. The main building was transformed first into a reception center for the wounded and, immediately after that, into a military hospital.

The living situation shared by the personnel of the

---

4   Cf. B. Calzolari, *L'Hotel Subasio specchio dei tempi Momenti di vita assisana dal 1868 in poi*, Assisi, Tip. Porziuncola, 1983, p. 157. The only representative of the Italian army in Assisi was Colonel Guido Manardi, later general of the Monte Rosa division, who took the initiative of creating a "Presidium command" (composed of himself) in Assisi, thus permitting the Germans to have an interlocutor in the city. (ibid.)

5   Editor's footnote: Today Casa Papa Giovanni.

6   Information received from Rev. Otello Migliosi.

home and the German military was proper, marked by mutual respect. There were cordial relations between the rector and the German Commander who, often commiserating with the conditions under which the people of the home were forced to live, ordered those under him to give the children medicine, school supplies and even food.

National Home for Orphans of Teachers,
Center of the second German military hospital in Assisi

Those first German divisions quickly revealed their arrogance and violence. Bearing witness to this was, among others, the Mayor of Assisi at that time, Arnaldo Fortini, who said:

One evening their commander, a captain of the Luftwaffe, called me to the Hotel Savoia where he was staying, and through an interpreter informed me of many bans to be imposed on the people, almost all of which were punishable by death—execution for whoever did not turn in their arms, for anyone committing sabotage, for anyone who perpetrated any activity against the German military, for anyone found in certain areas, etc. At the end he asked me for a certain number of hostages, to be taken from the more suspect elements.

I replied that no Italian could possibly agree to such a request and hand other Italians over to a foreign army, regardless of which army it may be, without bringing great shame upon himself. And since that captain insisted, I added that if he were in my place and under the same conditions, he would certainly have acted in the same way.

This calm but decisive statement seemed to have touched him. He replied that he appreciated my position and he was willing to renounce the idea of the hostages, on the condition that I would accept personal responsibility for whatever might occur. I agreed without hesitation; and thus it came about that not a single citizen of Assisi was deported, not a single one was executed or taken in reprisal.

On 15 October the Germans requisitioned the Theological College of the Friars Minor Conventual, menacingly asking the rector to hand over the keys to some storage areas immediately.[7] At three o'clock the following afternoon, German officers and soldiers, led by a Gestapo

---

7   Cf. Mansi, *Relazione*, p. 10.

officer, surrounded the Basilica of St. Francis and the Sacro Convento, blocking the exits, in order to check all the religious to see if there were any English or American soldiers hidden there.

They conducted "a thorough search of the whole convent. Entering part of the complex reserved to the sisters, the search teams found two articles of men's clothing and threatened the sisters with deportation to Germany and accusation before a military tribunal."[8] In reality they were clothes belonging to two men who worked in the convent gardens, as was proven by papers found in the pockets.[9]

After this awful experience the Custos hurriedly sent one of his confreres to Rome the following day, 17 October, "to inform the Father General of the search by the Germans and to ask the Holy See for a document of exemption from search and seizure."[10] On that same day, at the same hour as the day before, some German officers searched the Sacro Convento a second time, interrogating and studying the documents of all the foreign religious. This two-day investigation ended without incident, but "the whole city" was surprised "about the illegal action taken against the Basilica and the Sacro Convento, which are the property of the Holy See."[11]

On 19 October the governor of Vatican City, Marquis Serafini, was charged by the Secretary of State, Cardinal

---

8   Cf. Mani, p. 10.

9   Cf. P.S. Attal, *Assisi città santa. Come fu salvata dagli orrori della guerra*, in MISCELLANEA FRANCESCANA, 48 (948) I, pp. 11-12.

10   *Chronicle of the Sacro Convento.*

11   Ibid.

Luigi Maglione, to present to the German Military Authorities in Italy a document certifying that the Basilica and the buildings connected to it were the property of the Holy See and, as such, were exempt from any search or seizure.[12]

On 18 November the Apostolic Nuncio in Italy, Archbishop Francesco Borgongini Duca, sent Fr. Bede Hess, General Minister of the Friars Minor Conventual, the official declaration of the Holy See, confirmed by the German Military Authority, concerning the accord[13] on the basis of which the following notices could be posted to the doors of the Basilica, the Sacro Convento and other buildings belonging to them: "Proprietà della S. Sede. ESENTE. Eigentum des Heiligen Stuhles."[14]

However, saving Assisi from war and destruction was an entirely different matter. The religious and civil authorities had been working on this matter for some time.

HOW CAN ASSISI BE SAVED?[15]

In a brief analysis, one realizes that there were five persons especially involved in the effort to save the city of Assisi:

— the General Minister of the Friars Minor Conventual, Fr. Bede Hess;

---

12   Ibid.

13   Cf. Attal, p. 12.

14   Ibid. and *Chronicle of the Sacro Convento*. Trans. note: The signs declared, in Italian and German, "Property of the Holy See. Exempt."

15   Santucci, pp. 51-70, *Come salvare Assisi*. Used with permission. English translation by Nancy Celaschi, OSF.

— the Custos of the Sacro Convento, Fr. Bonaventura Mansi;
— the Bishop of Assisi, Bishop Giuseppe Placido Nicolini;
— the Mayor of Assisi, Arnaldo Fortini;
— the director of the German military hospitals in Assisi, Colonel Valentin Müller, MD

Although we know what would eventually be done to save Assisi would be the result of their joint effort and harmony, down to this very day it is difficult to state for certain which of these men made the first move, initiating the long, patient, tenacious and ultimately successful process. On this subject, Francesco Salvatore Attal writes:

Early in 1941 the Custos of the Sacro Convento, Fr. Bonaventure Mansi, OFM Conv, spoke to the Mayor of Assisi, Arnaldo Fortini, concerning the danger the city faced because of the presence in various places—including the Sala Norsa very near the Sacro Convento and dependent on it—of Italian recruits in training. This situation could result in some dangerous development by turning the city into an active military center, exposing it to the risks of war. Arnaldo Fortini, who had been administering the city astutely and with steadfast dedication, immediately understood what the Custos meant. Bishop Placido Nicolini, the well-loved ordinary, was informed of the situation as well and gave his full support to the initiatives being planned.

They decided to approach the Italian authorities

and insist that the recruits be removed, and institute instead a military convalescent hospital in Assisi. Also making a contribution to the success of the project was the late Colonel Alfred Baduel, MD, Director of the Hospital of Assisi. Thus, to the agreement of all, the convalescent hospital was opened at the Institute for the Blind and Deaf, just outside of Porta San Francesco. The Bishop sent the Sisters of St. Mary of the Angels there and appointed a chaplain. Thus the first danger was averted and no fighting divisions were lodged in Assisi.[16]

Arnaldo Fortini recalls the following:

> On Easter Monday 1942, while the people of Assisi were rendering their traditional homage of the veil of the Blessed Virgin who throughout the centuries had preserved the city from so many afflictions, in my capacity as Mayor of the city and President of the International Society of Franciscan Studies, I suggested to Fr Giuseppe Abate, himself a member of the same society and General Secretary of the Order of Friars Minor Conventual, the undertaking of direct action to save Assisi from conflict and destruction of war, confident that I was expressing the desire of peoples of all nations. This suggestion was also shared with the Custos of the Sacro Convento, Fr. Bonaventura Mansi.
>
> We had to overcome some very serious obstacles which arose because of our status as citizens of

---

16   Attal, pp. 4-5.

one of the countries at war, thus forbidden to have relations not only with the hostile states, but with neutral ones as well. Consequently we turned to Fr. Bede Hess, General Minister of the Friars Minor Conventual, who took the required steps to approach the Secretariat of State of the Holy See....[17]

Recalling the steps taken to safeguard Assisi, at the end of 1944 Bishop Nicolini in a memo sent to the military governor of the city, Lieutenant Garigue, stated: "First of all, the Custos of the Convento of San Francesco, encouraged by me, asked the Holy See to urge the ambassadors of the various nations at war to take an interest."[18]

However, it would be good to follow step-by-step the long journey of this cause, relying most of all on the documents available to us.[19]

Before studying the action taken through the Holy See and, through this action, appealing to the diplomatic or military representatives of the warring nations—and even to the heads of state of some of them—it should be noted that as early as 16 July 1943 the Franciscans at the Sacro Convento in Assisi, were concerned about protecting the tomb of St. Francis from any eventual damage caused by the advancing war. Therefore, they appealed to the Pope for authorization, asking him also to forbid the construction of

---

17   Fortini, p. 215. See also the BOLLETINO DELLA SOCIETÀ INTERNAZIONALE DI STUDI FRANCESCANI, 1946, fasc. XIV-XV-XVI, pp. 61-62.

18   Diocesan Archives of Assisi, Bishop Nicolini, autograph ms.

19   These documents are preserved in the archives of the Vatican Secretariat of State and that of the Order of Friars Minor Conventual in Rome which I (Santucci) consulted through published citations, as well as the Diocesan Archives of Assisi and the Archives of the Sacro Convento, which I consulted directly.

an underground chamber near the Basilica, which the civic authorities were planning for use as an air raid shelter.[20]

On 4 August the Apostolic Nuncio in Italy, Archbishop Francesco Borgongini Duca, replied: "The Holy Father had kindly deigned to grant the authorization for the work planned for the protection of the venerated tomb of the Seraphic Father" and he would also appeal to the Italian government to construct the chamber elsewhere.[21]

The next day Fr. Mansi left for Rome, summoned by the General Minister of the Order concerning the planned work, and on 6 August the same Minister informed the Nuncio that the Custos was in charge of preparing the plans for the protection of the saint's tomb. The work was entrusted to the architect, Mr. Ugo Tarchi.[22]

It should be pointed out here that the General Minister of the Order of Friars Minor Conventual was an American and had a personal acquaintance with the personal representative of the President of the United States of America to the Holy See, Mr. Myron C. Taylor, and knew the chargé d'affaires, Mr. Harold H. Tittmann, even better.[23]

It was to the latter gentleman that, on 7 August 1943, Fr. Bede Hess gave an explanatory document in which he asked the United States government to intervene so that the Basilica of St. Francis and the whole city of Assisi might

---

20   Cf. Mansi, p. 9.

21   Cf. Attal, pp. 8-9. Meanwhile, the air raid shelter was never built.

22   *Chronicle of the Sacro Convento.*

23   Cf. Attal, p. 9.

be saved from "ground or air attack."[24]

The official letter of Fr. Bede Hess ended as follows:

> As General Superior of the Franciscan Order of Friars Minor Conventual to whom the care of the Sacred Basilica is entrusted, in the name of all the followers and admirers of St. Francis and as an American citizen who, next to God, passionately loves his country, I strongly ask you to request our government to issue an order to our ground and air forces that the Sacred Basilica of St. Francis of Assisi should be saved for its historical, architectural and artistic value, because it is papal property in the custody of my Order, because it is an object of affection and veneration for millions of followers and admirers of the Saint including the United States of America, and because there are no military installations in Assisi.[25]

However, the Custos of the Basilica did not let up, and while the General Minister was in Assisi from 13-18 August, he informed Fr. Hess that there was continued danger of a "militarization of Assisi as an arms and munitions depot." He asked him to notify the Holy See so that such a threat would be removed far from the city.[26]

In the interim, Mr. Tarchi had drawn up plans for protecting the tomb of St Francis and on 25 August the Custos sent them to Italy's Minister of Public Works.

---

24   Cf. *Chronicle of the Sacro Convento.*

25   Attal, p. 9.

26   *Chronicle of the Sacro Convento.*

However, Minister Allicata informed him that, following upon the events of 25 July, all work on the Sacro Convento was suspended.[27]

On 2 September the Vatican Secretariat of State replied to the requests and concerns expressed by Fr. Bede Hess, stating that the "fear of military measures (planned) for Assisi" was "absolutely groundless."[28]

Concerning the tunnel to be excavated next to St. Francis Basilica, the Vatican Secretariat of State on 9 September informed the Father General that the Minister of the Interior had instructed the Prefect of Perugia to "suspend all plans regarding the construction of a tunnel in Assisi, which was to be dug in the territory of the Sacro Convento."[29]

In early autumn 1943, as we have already noted, a German military hospital was opened in Assisi. On 3 November the new head of the Province of Perugia, Dr. Armando Rocchi, notified the Military Regional Command and the Mayors about this in a note which stated: "The German Command of Piazza di Perugia has stipulated that, following the preparation of a German field hospital in Assisi, the sick or wounded German soldiers can no longer be admitted to Italian civil and military hospitals."[30]

On 4 December 1943 the Holy See began the paper work to have Assisi recognized and declared as a "hospital city, the only way to save the whole city from the horrors of

---

27   Ibid.

28   Ibid.

29   Ibid.

30   No. 8917 of the Cabinet of the Prefecture of Perugia.

the war."[31]

On the basis of the suggestions offered by Fr. Mansi, Fr. Bede Hess presented to the Cardinal Secretary of State "a detailed explanation with particular information" regarding the war situation "which was being determined in Assisi."[32] Since this document is of fundamental importance, it would be good to quote the text almost in its entirety:[33]

> Two German military hospitals have been established in Assisi, one in the Prince of Naples Home and the other in the new buildings of the Institute for the Deaf, Dumb and Blind, quite near the Basilica. Other buildings in various parts of the city complete the hospital structure. The Subasio, Giotto and Savoia Hotels, all very near the Basilica, house German officers and troops. The airfields of Foligno and Perugia, the latter just a few kilometers from Assisi, have already been affected by recent fighting.
>
> Airplanes from both sides continually fly over Assisi, striking the surrounding areas. There is real justification for concern about preserving the artistic, historic and religious patrimony of the Basilica and the whole city of Assisi. Any damage to this heritage would be an irreparable loss and would be deplored by the whole civilized world which loves the city of St. Francis as a symbol of peace and love,

---

31 *Chronicle of the Sacro Convento.*

32 Ibid.

33 Attal, pp. 12-14.

recognizing its absolute lack of military purpose.

Therefore the same measures should be adopted for Assisi as have been adopted for Florence. From an artistic and historical viewpoint alone, functionaries of the Ministry for National Education, with specific functions, have made the first contacts with German military authorities, who have demonstrated their willingness to pass on to their High Command the reasons for preserving Assisi from eventual damage in the war.

I therefore ask Your Eminence to look into the possibility of a diplomatic initiative on the part of the Secretariat of State of the Supreme Pontiff, Pius XII, with the ambassadors of Germany, England and the United States of America, so that the whole city of Assisi may be preserved from wartime harm by all of the armies in battle. If the action of the Ministers of National Education has been considered just and opportune and kindly received because of the care and conservation of the vast, priceless, historic, artistic patrimony of the city of Assisi, we trust that the action of the supreme ecclesiastical authority will meet with the highest consideration because of the spiritual importance and the sacred character of the Seraphic City. With such a wealth of religious memorials and shrines, it is venerated throughout the Catholic world and visited by persons of every nation and religion.

Let it also be noted that the Basilica and the Sacro

Convento and the related buildings situated in various parts of the city of Assisi are the property of the Holy See, recognized as such by the Concordat of 11 February 1929. Only a commitment agreed upon by all the authorities of the parties at war can save the city of St. Francis from the damage and destruction of the war and fulfill the commitment already undertaken by the German military authorities to respect the property of the Holy See in Assisi.

Since it is held that the presence of two German hospitals in Assisi does not constitute an obstacle to an agreement between the various parties at war, with the city being used for purposes of a medical nature, all that is required is for the various parties to agree to keep the city of Assisi free from military commands of active troops, temporary military commands and passing troops, from storage of arms and military materiel, from artillery or antiaircraft emplacements, from stationing of troops and from offensive or defensive lines, and of any type of military action which leads to damage, devastation, fire or looting.

Such provisions would avert direct offensives. However, it would also be necessary to ensure that any zone of military operations which would eventually be established would be at such a distance as to prevent indirect damage caused by collapse or destruction which can happen so easily due to displacement of air in centuries-old buildings, especially the Basilica, which is built on the side of a geologically faulted hill and has already been subject to many serious fissures.

> Bowing to offer you homage,
> Fr. Bede M. Hess, OFM Conv.
> General Minister

After this memo, Fr. Bede sent some informational material, the most significant of which reads as follows:[34]

1. In addition to the two German military hospitals, other buildings have been requisitioned and occupied in various parts of the city so that Assisi is taking on an increasingly military character, the development of which we cannot foresee.

2. Many officials and pilots of the airfield of Perugia, closer to Assisi, are being lodged in the Hotels Subasio, Giotto and Savoia, from which they leave and to which they return after air raids. Such hotels close to the Basilica could draw hostile air bombardment.

3. Squads of workers from Assisi are requisitioned each day and taken to the nearby airfield for military work. The greater effectiveness of the camp itself for defensive action and placement of arms constitutes a serious threat to Assisi.

Added to this was railway and road traffic—almost entirely of a military nature, danger of the possibility of storing

---

34 Ibid., p. 14.

munitions in the basement of the military hospitals, searches conducted by the Germans, trouble frequently caused by drunken German soldiers and their numerous threats to blow everything up should they have to retreat so that it could not be used by the enemy.[35]

All this was meant to emphasize the drama of the situation to the Vatican Secretariat of State so that the Holy See might take the necessary measures and avoid even greater risks to Assisi.

On 28 December the General Minister wrote to the Custos of the Sacro Convento, notifying him that the paperwork for the protection of Assisi presented to the Holy See was taking promising turns, but it was necessary for the local civil and military authorities to indicate "the reasons" necessary "for the salvation of Assisi."[36] And so on 4 January 1944 the Custos asked Arnaldo Fortini "to prepare a statement to present to the highest authority in Italy for the protection of Assisi."[37]

In mentioning his own interventions, Fortini would later write that this step was taken upon the initiative of the International Society for Franciscan Studies, which for more than 40 years had its headquarters in Assisi, and of

---

35   Ibid., pp.14-15.

36   *Chronicle of the Sacro Convento.*

37   Ibid. Although retaining the title of Mayor of Assisi, Fortini had de facto been replaced, for reasons of health, by the commissary of the prefecture, Dr. Francesco Paolo Gargiulo. Fortini would resign definitively from the office of Mayor of Assisi on 1 March 1944. On the 12th of the same month the provincial leader, Dr. Armando Rocchi, would name Mr. Alcide Checconi, who would remain in that office until 9 June 1944.

which he had been president for more than 40 years.[38] Fortini writes:[39] "Since we ourselves could not make any direct appeal to Vatican City, it was decided that our official proposal to have Assisi declared an open, hospital city, would be addressed to the government of the Socialist Republic, and that an authenticated copy of this proposal would be sent to the Vatican Secretariat of State."

This did happen, and once again it was Fr. Hess who saw to it that Fortini's letter did arrive at the Secretariat of State.[40]

Concerning this topic, on 20 January 1944 the chronicler of the Sacro Convento noted: "Fortini has prepared the civil statement for the protection of Assisi. The statement is addressed to H.E. Benito Mussolini, Head of the Government of the Italian Socialist Republic."[41] Here follows the complete text of the Mayor's appeal:

> In my capacity as Mayor of the city of Assisi[42] and as President of the International Society of Franciscan Studies, I believe it is my duty to submit for your examination the situation in Assisi regarding the unfolding and current operations relating to the war.
>
> Assisi, the heart of the world, is the birthplace of St. Francis and the one city which, after Rome and Jerusalem, because of its tradition of holiness, its artistic treasures and its most noble significance

---

38   Fortini, p. 216.

39   Ibid.

40   Ibid.

41   Ibid.

42   Since 1923.

whence Dante was given to salute it as the *Novissimo Oriente*, shines brightly on the heights of the human spirit, but today is threatened by the war which is knocking at its doors.

The wonderful church built over the bodily remains of the Seraphic Saint which a great writer, Adolfo Venturi, called "the most beautiful house of prayer of which the earth can boast," is already caught up in a whirlpool of the battle which, because of frequent aerial bombardments, has already claimed a great number of victims and destroyed important monuments in the surrounding area, from Perugia to Foligno.

And with the famous triple Basilica, immortalized by Cimabue, Giotto and Simone Martini, other Franciscan churches are likewise in danger: San Damiano, the Porziuncola, the Cathedral, the Bishop's house, Santa Maria Sopra Minerva.

It is useless to try to indicate what a loss it would be to people of every nation if any of these masterpieces, not only of art but more so of the spirit, were to be lost!

And indeed, as if by a tacit and instinctive homage to the highest ideals of beauty and goodness which smile upon human hearts, even when they are in mortal combat, the band of iron and fire has reached the threshold of the holy city, over which hundreds of fighter planes fly daily.

We therefore request that, similar to what has

happened for Rome, this situation be confirmed de jure, by which the various nations at war would commit themselves or at least confirm their desire to spare Assisi and the neighboring Franciscan monuments.

It should be kept in mind that the city's fame is of a purely mystical and spiritual nature and that it has absolutely no importance politically (it has only 5,000 inhabitants), industrially (there are no factories within its walls), militarily (there are no forts or troop commands), topographically (it is far from major roads and its rail station, situated on the secondary line from Foligno to Terontola, is five kilometers away from the city).

On the other hand for centuries the faithful from every nation have come on pilgrimage (for the centenary of Francis in 1926 two million visitors from every nation came); the many convents and monasteries (including one monastery each of English, American, Bavarian, Spanish, and French nuns, not to mention the general headquarters of the most flourishing international missionary associations—the Missionaries of Egypt, Gesù Bambino, del Giglio and the Minors Conventual— who have always performed their work in all parts of the world to ease the suffering of people of every country and race); the admiration and veneration of those who love art, from every country, have by now made it an international center of culture and faith, to which all hearts pay homage, without distinction.

Let us note that for more than 40 years the city has been the headquarters of the International Society for Franciscan Studies, founded by the Frenchman Paul Sabatier, and later presided over by the Dane, Joergensen, the Englishman Cuthbert, and today by the undersigned, to which scholars from all nations have given their full participation and collaboration.

Lastly, it should be observed that the Basilica and Sacro Convento of San Francesco (almost one fourth of the whole city), the Conventual Missionary College and the Theological Seminary belong to the Holy See, so that even the German military authorities have already made a direct commitment to the Holy See concerning those buildings to refrain from executing acts of occupation or simple search; that other buildings, such as the Basilica of St. Clare and the Patriarchal Basilica of Saint Mary of the Angels, are under the direct jurisdiction of the Supreme Pontiff.

We ask that opportune measures be taken so that the nations party to the war agree that the Franciscan monuments and the city should be immune from aerial or artillery bombardment, and that there be no offensive or defensive emplacements in it, nor stores of ammunition or military materiel or troop commands, although there could be space for hospitals for the wounded.

Arnaldo Fortini [43]

---

43   The text of Fortini's letter appeared in Bolletino della Società Internazionale

Indeed, the German army did need other buildings. Thus on 17 January 1944 the German Command asked the Sacro Convento for the complex of the Theological College, located on the Via del Seminario, but received a firm refusal from the Conventuals.[44]

> The same building was requested once again as a residence and placement for the paratroopers. The request was a dramatic one—as can be read in the report of 27 January: 'they got the Bishop to urge us to give in. When we responded that it is the property of the Holy See they required us to telephone the Holy See and give them an answer by ten o'clock the following day, the 28th, or else they would requisition all the other buildings on via San Francesco, very near the Basilica. However, we did not give in this time. To make the story short,' Fr. Mansi continues, 'let it suffice to say here that approximately fifteen times they asked for the use of the Theological College, sometimes for military use, other times for housing evacuees. We are certain that our refusal made an effective contribution to preventing the militarization of Assisi and eliminating obstacles, which would have been insurmountable at a later date, to naming Assisi a hospital city and thus to the salvation of the city and the evacuees.'[45]

Thus we have the point of view of the Custos at that time.

DI STUDI FRANCESCANI, 1946, fasc. XIV-XV-XVI, pp. 62-64; in Fortini, op cit, pp. 216-218; in Attal, op cit., pp. 15-16.

44   Cf. *Chronicle of the Sacro Convento.*

45   Mansi, p. 10.

Today, many years later, we feel that Fr. Mansi was right in denying the use of the Theological College for military purposes, but we fail to see his motives in denying the use of that structure for housing evacuees.

However, the praiseworthy work of the Conventuals was continuing on another front—the application for the salvation of Assisi. On 5 February, in fact, the Custos presented the following:

> A new, more thorough statement to the Holy See concerning the protection of Assisi. In this new document the Holy See was informed of other buildings in Assisi which the Germans had requisitioned for military purposes and of their violent attempt on 27 January to occupy our Theological College, despite its status of exemption from requisition. There is talk of requisitioning the Umbrian Regional Seminary. Thus we can see that requisition of civilian buildings will be followed by requisition of religious ones, but even if this does not happen, the presence of operational troops quartered in civilian buildings in Assisi would constitute a grave threat to the religious buildings, sanctuaries and Franciscan monuments of the Seraphic City. The statement ended with a request that the Holy See hasten recognition of Assisi as a hospital city, observing the three points which follow:
>
> 1. That the resolve be retained by which it was agreed not to requisition buildings which are the property of the Holy See and not to militarize

the whole city of Assisi, due to its mystical, spiritual, historical and artistic nature.

2. That if, because of a need to increase the number of hospitals, the Holy See would decide to allow use of the religious buildings it owns, the occupants would commit themselves to using the buildings as hospitals only, not transforming them into military housing and promising to return them immediately if they are no longer used as hospitals.

3. That the military authorities who are granted the use of religious buildings for hospitals must commit themselves not to requisition civic buildings for other purposes, so that Assisi can become a city destined exclusively for use as a hospital. Indeed, it is obvious that it would be a grave error if religious buildings of Assisi were to be used as hospitals and the civil buildings as army barracks. This would make Assisi a military objective and would bring ruin down on the whole city.[46]

While the *Chronicle of the Sacro Convento* reveals that the author of the statement is the Custos, Fr. Mansi, in reality the long petition bears the signature of the General Minister, Fr. Bede Hess,[47] who, after first mentioning his previous appeal of 4 December 1943 and recalling that the Mayor had appealed to the Government of the Republic of

---

46   *Chronicle of the Sacro Convento.*

47   See the document in Attal, pp. 17-21.

Italy, makes his own the ideas which had obviously been suggested to him by Fr. Mansi.

At a certain point in the statement Fr. Hess recalls that the head of the Province of Perugia, in a recent conversation with the Bishop of Assisi, Giuseppe Placido Nicolini:

> offered his own proposal, saying that if Assisi does not want to have military garrisons or operational troops, it would have to increase the number of German hospitals in order to receive a greater number of the sick and wounded. 'Therefore he proposed,' this according to Fr. Bede in his statement, 'the opening of a third German hospital, and would present a formal request within a few days time. The place designated for that new hospital is the Theological Missionary College of the Friars Minor Conventual, which is the property of the Holy See.... 'The Bishop of Assisi, for his part,' as Fr. Bede continues to write, 'since he is the Delegate for the Sacred Congregation for Seminaries and Universities for the Regional Seminary of Umbria located in Assisi, said that he is willing to cede the Regional Seminary for another hospital after Easter, unless he receives orders to the contrary from his superiors.'

However, at this point we should make an observation. The head of the Province, Dr. Rocchi, was correct. In order to save Assisi from the German troops, it would be necessary to open a third hospital (the first two were, the reader may recall, the Institute for the Blind and the National Home for Orphans of Teachers). And the Bishop had understood this.

He was willing to grant the use of the Regional Seminary for this purpose, something which he would eventually do without even consulting the Vatican, the legal owner of the buildings, and thus incurring the dissatisfaction of Cardinal Pizzardo.[48]

However, from Fr. Hess' statement we see that the Conventuals had not understood this:

> It can be seen that the two large German military hospitals already existing in Assisi, capable of housing almost 2,000 wounded, would have fulfilled the duty of the Seraphic City to contribute to the needs of the war and are already enough to obtain Assisi's classification as a hospital city.
>
>
>
> At this point we would do well to insert into the intricate and convulsive tangle of events in that period the figure of the physician, Colonel Valentin Müller, Commander of the German Armed Forces, to assume the direction of the German hospitals in the city from the beginning of February 1944.[49]

Colonel Valentin Müller (1891-1951)

---

48   This was confirmed by Don Aldo Brunacci, who at that time was in the Vatican, having undergone an investigation on charges of suspected anti-Fascism by Dr. Rocchi, head of the Province.

49   Cf. Attal, p. 21.

However, we know that Müller was already present in the city on 5 December 1943, when a concert of spiritual music was held in the *Sala Gotica* of the Sacro Convento, directed by Fr. Domenico Stella, with the collaboration of the musical cappella of the Basilica.

On that occasion the Bishop of Assisi was seated next to Müller. The singer was an evacuee, the soprano Susanna Dango. Accompanying her on the piano was another evacuee, a man from Palermo, who had a surname that was rather risky for those times, Maestro Franco Ferrara.[50]

From that moment on, Müller's presence in Assisi would be a decisive contribution to the rapid conclusion of the plan to save the city.

His frequent meetings with the Custos of St. Francis' Basilica, (Catholic that he was, he attended daily Mass and Communion) convinced him that if Assisi was to be declared a hospital city, it would be necessary to evacuate all the German soldiers still located there.

All the other authorities of the city prodded him in this as well. First of all, Bishop Nicolini, who did so every time he invited him to dinner in the Bishop's residence or was at his side for various religious or civic celebrations in the city. And Müller did manage to convince the German authorities to remove the German military police from the

---

50   *Chronicle of the Sacro Convento.* Both Dango and Ferrara would hold another concert in Assisi, this one at the Theological College on 12 March 1944. Exactly one month after the first concert, on 6 January 1944, Colonel Müller dined with the Bishop, who was celebrating his birthday (information furnished by Fr. Otello Migliosi, former chancellor of the diocese).

Hotel Giotto and the aviators from the Hotel Subasio.[51]

ASSISI: A HOSPITAL CITY[52]

From that time on Assisi was truly a hospital city and nothing else, and Colonel Valentin Müller was not only director of the hospitals but also military commander of the piazza.

In the interim, Fr. Mansi's tireless work continued. Colonel Müller had told him: "You continue your work, and I'll do what I can on my part."[53]

In March 1944, for example, when the Custos of the Sacro Convento went to Padua to meet the new Director of Fine Arts for the Ministry of National Education, Prof. Carlo Anti, concerning the protection of Assisi and its artistic treasures, he asked the Minister to take the necessary steps in the Italian government to have Assisi declared a hospital city.[54]

Fortini had earlier made a similar request to Minister Biggini.[55]

At the same time the ceaseless but subtle work of the Vatican continued, and on 24 April 1944 the Secretariat of State informed the Sacro Convento that the request to have Assisi declared a hospital city was proceeding and it seemed

---

51   Attal, p. 21.

52   Santucci, pp. 70-79, *Assisi "Città Ospedaliera"*. Used with permission. English translation by Nancy Celaschi, OSF.

53   Ibid.

54   Ibid. and the *Chronicle of the Sacro Convento*.

55   Cf. Attal, p. 22.

that the desired results would be obtained before long.[56] On 24 April 1944 the Vatican Secretary of State, Cardinal Luigi Maglione, informed the General Minister that he had received and studied his statement of 5 February and all the parties at war were also examining the situation. On 28 April the General Minister communicated this to the Custos, once again expressing the wish that this recognition would be granted soon.[57] This was the last letter that arrived in Assisi before the Anglo-American occupation of the city.[58]

Also concerned with the absolute demilitarization of the city was the commissioner, Mr. Checconi, who on 25 April 1944 sent a private communiqué to the German Commander of the Piazza, Colonel Müller, noting the following:

> Enclosed is a statement from the Abbess of the Monastery of St. Clare in which she complains that the German military has stored some 120 drums of petroleum near the sanctuary and many military vehicles park under the arches of the Basilica and the adjacent piazza.
>
> I must take this occasion to point out the danger caused by the presence of mobile radio transmitters in various parts of the city.
>
> I must also point out that the custodian of the medieval Rocca has informed me that in recent days German troops, despite the fact that they have seen the notice installed by Gen. Kesserling (sic)

56   Cf. Mansi, p. 11.

57   Cf. *Chronicle of the Sacro Convento.*

58   Cf. Attal, p. 23.

declaring the fortress a national monument under the protection of the German command, have installed a telephone line from the large tower to the small tower of the fortress itself. This certainly gives the impression that the monument may also be utilized by the German armed forces.

I have taken the liberty of pointing out these things because I know of your concern for the patients in these military hospitals and I think that their interest coincides with that of the religious and artistic heritage of this city, which is today predominantly a hospital city.[59]

Fr. Mansi could still not rest easy, and on 9 May he received permission from the German military command in Italy to go to Florence "to confer with the Ministry of Culture concerning questions about Assisi."[60] Under the date of Saturday, 17 May, we read in the *Chronicle of the Sacro Convento*:

In Florence the Custos conferred with the Colonel and with Dr. Langsdorff, German Head of Office for the Care of Art in Italy. Present for the discussions were the Director of the Institute for the History of German Art and the Superintendent of the Galleries of Florence, Dr. Giovanni Poggi. The Custos informed the Colonel of the exemption of

---

59   Personal archives of Bruno Calzolari. The placement of Division n.56068, which the German Armed Forces positioned at the Giotto Hotel on 19 April 1944 did not constitute a provocation for the Allies, perhaps because it passed unobserved. Ibid.

60   *Chronicle of the Sacro Convento.*

the Basilica from any search or requisition since it is the property of the Holy See, recognized as such by the German Supreme Command. The Custos also asked the Colonel to intervene with the proper German authorities to hasten recognition of Assisi as a 'hospital city,' and that precise indications concerning this be given to Colonel Müller, German Commander of the hospitals of Assisi. This was not only in relation to Assisi's historic importance but also because of the new depository of the works of art that had been created there. The German Colonel assured the Custos that the very next day he would send the Supreme Command of the German Forces in Italy a report totally in favor of his request.[61]

Besides the Custos and Prof. Alexander Langsdorff, the meeting was attended by Dr. Heinrich Heydenreich, Director of the German Institute of the History of Art in Florence and director of the department for the care of art in Tuscany and Umbria.[62] At the same time Colonel Müller was doing his part, designating other buildings of the city for use as military hospitals. Besides the Locatelli Palace, the Seraphic Institute for the Deaf, Dumb and Blind, the National Home for Orphans of Teachers and the Umbrian Regional Seminary would house wounded German soldiers.[63] On 5 June the superiors of the Sacro Convento decided to give Colonel Müller the use of the upper floor

---

61   Ibid.

62   Cf. Attal, p. 23.

63   Cf. A. Brunacci, *L'opera di assistenza del clero e del vescovo di Assisi dopo l'8 settembre 1943 in Cattolici e fascisti in Umbria (1922-1945)*, A. Monticone, ed. Bologna, Il Mulino, 1978, p. 453.

of the Theological College to establish a hospital section there.[64] By this time things were ready to have Assisi declared a "hospital city." In fact, all the conditions had been met. The Holy See had been very much involved in advancing this with the Allied governments. The German command was directly interested in such recognition to guarantee the safety of the thousands of wounded being treated in the hospitals of Assisi. Even the Italian government (although obviously it did not carry much weight in any decision-making on the matter) had been asked several times for such recognition. Now the city was truly a hospital city, and nothing else.

And of course, there was the art to safeguard, and everyone was aware of this—the Germans, the Vatican, the Anglo-Americans (we need only recall the art collection of the famous American art critic, F.M. Perkins, had been brought to the Sacro Convento).[65]

In the second half of May the news had spread. The radio had announced that Assisi had been proclaimed an "open city." However, as we shall see, that was not exactly true.[66]

Regardless of the fact of whether or not that rumor was true, on 19 May the British representative to the Holy See gave the assurance that for his government's part, "although not disposed to proceed with the above-mentioned recognition, it would assume precaution for the safety of the hospitals and artistic treasures of the Seraphic City and that very

---

64   Cf. Mansi, p. 11.

65   In this regard see the chapter dedicated to the protection of cultural goods. Perkins would later donate a collection of 57 paintings to the Sacro Convento.

66   Cf. Attal, p. 24.

strict instructions to that effect had been given to the commanders of the Allied air forces."[67]

On 30 May in a letter numbered b. 7985/S, Bishop Giovanni Battista Montini of the Vatican Secretariat of State, wrote to Fr. Bede Hess, asking him to communicate this to the Custos of the Sacro Convento. However, because of the difficulties of that period, the letter never reached Assisi.[68] In fact, there is no trace of it in the archives of the Sacro Convento. Thus the Vatican's work had been crowned with success. In just a little while the efforts on the other front—the German front—would also yield their desired effect.

On 31 May, in fact, the German Ambassador to the Holy See, "in reply to the notes numbered 78066/S of 24 April and 2549/44 of 5 May concerning the city of Assisi," communicated: "the 'Generalissimo'[69] of the German Forces in Italy has consented to Assisi being declared a 'hospital city.' According to his declaration, at present there is nothing in Assisi except field hospitals and medical units. The same Generalissimo has prohibited the occupation of the city of Assisi by other troops or commands of the *Wehrmacht*."[70]

The greatly desired news, however, communicated by the Secretariat of State, reached Assisi only on 21 June, after the city's liberation, in a letter from Cardinal Maglione

---

67   Ibid. and Fortini, p. 219.

68   Cf. Attal, p. 24.

69   An obvious reference to Kesselring.

70   Cf. Attal, p. 24 and Fortini, p. 219.

addressed to Fr. Bede Hess.[71] However, some people in Assisi must have been aware of this matter. On 31 May Colonel Müller went with four officers to give verbal communication of this news to Bishop Nicolini.[72] It was during that meeting that Colonel Müller asked Bishop Nicolini, the Holy See's delegate for the Umbrian Regional Seminary, for the use of that large complex just below Assisi on the old road to the Porziuncola.

Although the Bishop knew he should have first asked the Holy See, the owner of the complex, for such permission, he nonetheless told the German Colonel that he could certainly house wounded German soldiers in the seminary. As we have noted before, when news of that concession reached the Vatican, it provoked the wrath of Cardinal Giuseppe Pizzardo, Prefect of the Sacred Congregation for Seminaries.

The Bishop's decision was critical for Assisi's safety. If, in fact, the regional seminary had not been conceded for the care of the wounded, it would have certainly been requisitioned by the SS or other German troops. That would have inevitably provoked a reaction from the Allies, and thus the bombing of the area immediately adjacent to the city. Therefore, in the afternoon of 3 June 1944, the Umbrian Regional Seminary received is first wounded German soldiers.[73]

Another decisive action of the Bishop to remove the threat

---

71   Cf. Attal, p. 24.

72   Cf. Brunacci, p. 453.

73   Cf. V. Falcinelli, Torgiano, I. Lavoro - Religione - Folclore, S. Maria degli Angeli, Tip. Porziuncola 1977, p. 432.

of Allied bombing was that "several times he used" all his influence to "prevent the occupation of the house of Mr. Tibetio Gualdi by the German military forces,"[74] since that villa was situated right at Assisi's gates, on the road to Santa Maria degli Angeli.

That is precisely how things developed. For some time a German division had been lodged there, but they were officially used for medical work, taking care of the treatment of the German wounded. In reality, however, more than once the Allied airplanes heading for the airfield of Sant'Egidio were greeted by antiaircraft fire from Villa Gualdi.

This fact was noted especially by Mr. Gualdi, who had been forced to let the Germans use his villa. He himself lived across the street in another house he owned. And so, as the gentleman himself later recounted the events, he went to the Bishop's residence and reported this to Bishop Nicolini. The Bishop called Colonel Müller, who saw to it that the German division was immediately removed from Villa Gualdi, and he placed another small hospital there.

Several days before his meeting with Bishop Nicolini, Colonel Müller went to Foligno for a meeting with Marshall Kesselring, who had established his headquarters there.[75]

On that occasion Kesselring had informed him that things were going well for Assisi's recognition as a hospital city. But

---

74   AVA, Bishop Nicolini fund, a. 1944, b. Periodico bellico. Actually, that villa was supposed to be officially "used for the lodging of German troops," as can be read in an undated dispatch sent from Munich (Bruno Calzolari archives).

75   Cf. A. Bowl, *Order of the Day*, London, Leo Cooper, 1974, p. 98.

Müller expressed his concern that the retreating German troops might occupy the city. Kesselring then informed him that he would issue a special order forbidding German military troops from entering Assisi.[76]

Müller's generous and self-sacrificing work, however, was not yet finished. When, in fact, the first retreating German troops arrived on the plain below Assisi, the Colonel placed guards around the clock at all the gates of the city, using his own hospital personnel, to prevent the German troops from entering the city.[77]

Müller also had a barricade placed at Santa Maria degli Angeli, also near Santa Maria delle Grazie, to make the last retreating German troops understand that they were not to go up to Assisi.[78] Indeed, Müller knew that Assisi's salvation depended on the city remaining completely demilitarized until the front had completely passed it by.

As the Anglo-American troops drew nearer, during the second week of June, Müller received orders to evacuate the 2,000 German wounded and the hospital personnel from Assisi. He took personal command of the whole operation to make sure that no harm was done to anything that was being abandoned—buildings, furnishings, equipment.

The convoy of the wounded left the city on the morning of 15 June and Müller entrusted it to the command of his assistant. He wanted to remain in Assisi until the very last

---

76   Ibid.

77   Ibid.

78   Information furnished by Mr. Carmelo Piazza, a resident of Santa Maria degli Angeli.

moment.

The Allies were already on the plain between Foligno and Rivotorto. The German rear guard arrived that very same day at Santa Maria degli Angeli. There was a risk that those German soldiers might come up to Assisi to set up positions. Müller alone was capable of averting that danger. It is true that there were very exact promises not to do that, made by Kesselring the previous month, but there was still a danger. Moreover, the rear guard was a battalion of SS troops, known for their atrocities and autonomy. If they had decided to go to Assisi it would be the end of all the diplomatic efforts which had been going on for ten months. In fact, the presence of SS troops in Assisi would have inevitably provoked an Allied attack upon the city.

Therefore, as night fell on 15 June, Müller positioned himself outside the main gate of Assisi. From the valley he heard the sounds of demolition and could see the striking images of buildings set afire by the angry SS troops.

The next day some of the SS troops came up to Assisi. Müller and they began a heated debate, but the verbal exchange did not last long. It was long enough, however, for him to convince the German rear guard to abandon the city. Assisi was safe!

Shortly after midnight on 16 June Colonel Müller and his division set out on the road leading north.[79]

---

79   Cf. Bowl, pp. 99-100.

THE LIBERATION[80]

Before retreating the Germans mined and exploded the villa at Colle dei Benzi near Viole, the Costanzi mill at Santa Maria degli Angeli, also the bridge over the Chiascio at Petrignano d'Assisi.

On the morning of 17 June the Allies, coming from Foligno on the road through Viole, entered Assisi. But they arrived in tanks and personnel carriers, thus violating the city's "hospital" status, although it should be remembered that the aforementioned status had been conferred by the unilateral decision of the Germans.

Concerning those dramatic last hours, so decisive for Assisi's safety, we have these brief notes taken from the *Chronicle of the Sacro Convento*:[81]

16 Friday: During the night the English began bombardments in the valley, and they drew closer. The Assisians and all the others ran to the tomb of the Saint and, along with the religious, repeatedly recited the rosary and other prayers. Under these dreadful circumstances the tomb and the lower Basilica were turned into a public dormitory, as it were.

17 June: Around 9:30 this morning the Anglo-American troops entered Assisi by means of the Porta Nova and Porta Santa Chiara, passed through

---

80   Santucci, pp. 79-92. *La Liberazione*. Used with permission. English translation by Nancy Celaschi, OSF.

81   Archives of the Sacro Convento, ms.

the city, came through the lower piazza and stopped on the level area where they opened fire. From the surrounding hillsides the Germans returned their fire, hitting a few houses and a grenade also struck the bastion of Sixtus IV. There was no significant damage, however. All of Assisi was draped with banners and the bells sounded. Our Basilica kept out of the manifestations because this was the most delicate time for its safety.

In the afternoon the German artillery barrage continued, and the Anglo-American forces returned their fire. The people sought refuge in the Basilica.[82]

Of interest also are these notes from the *Chronicle of the Protoconvent* at Rivotorto concerning the day before the liberation:

16 June: At about five o'clock in the evening the bells were tolling for the funeral of the deceased Carmela Ronca and, as is our custom, the bell tolling was prolonged. Suddenly there was automatic weapons fire against the door of the convent and the community was alarmed. Father Leo, who was talking with some men against the wall of the first arcade of the cloister, was not immediately aware of the danger, but then as the gunfire was repeated, he and the men took refuge in the storage area where wood is kept, an area whose door opens onto the main highway. From there he called to Fr. Alessandro who was in his room on the upper floor, so that from

---

82   Ibid.

his window overlooking the main door he could call down to the soldiers and explain the situation to them. However, without any warning the scene changed. Fr. Leo, followed by the others, left his refuge. Upon seeing this, Fr. Alessandro climbed up into the tower, removed the ladder, and lay down flat in a hidden corner of the roof to wait and see what happened. About an hour passed until he heard Fr. Leo calling him from one of the windows in the bell tower. Fr. Leo was pale and shaking. Fr. Alessandro realized that something terrible had happened to him. There was no time to waste on explanations. Rather, they must immediately remove the Papal flag that was flying above the church. This could only be done by means of a ladder within the bell tower. What had happened?

The Germans had tried unsuccessfully to break down the main door, so they began working on the side door, and they had guessed correctly. However, the refugees had succeeded in making their way into the convent by the main stairway. So Fr. Leo decided to go to the soldiers and explain. Therefore, they went down the internal stairway and went through the church and there they met the soldiers. A voice shouted out to them that they were being accused of treason because of the tolling of the bells, the flag flying over the church and the closed doors. No explanations were accepted. They are "traitors" and must pay the price. They forced them to line up and aimed their rifles at them. But Fr. Leo was not about to die without trying to explain their innocence, and then explained, as best he could, their three imagined "crimes." He begged and pleaded with them, but it was all in vain. However, only one soldier was moved by the priest's pleas, and succeeded in persuading the others of their innocence. The adventure closed with a few kicks and the categorical command to remove the flag immediately. Besides Fr. Leo, the condemned included parishioners Giuseppe Salucci, Artemio Capitini and Enzo Gubbiotti. By seven o'clock everything was peaceful.

There were no more tanks or personnel carriers. No more soldiers. Some explosions could be heard in the area of Santa Maria degli Angeli and nothing more. This was a sure sign that we were in territory that for now was free and that in a short time we would be the prey of the advancing troops.

In the darkness of the night we could see clearly the fires coming from Montecatini and the Costanzi mill and an immense German tank which had been set afire by the retreating troops some 200 meters away from the church. Perhaps it was these fires that caused the Allies to turn their cannons on us, because at eleven o'clock a terrible bombardment began. It lasted for two hours. The two priests and two men from the parish (young Umberto Lena and Carmelo Giannuzzi had been sent to Assisi to the Theological College) did not take this seriously, since they thought they were explosions coming from munitions in the burning tank. Therefore, throughout the worst of the explosions, as the windows were shattered and stones and plaster fell, they were rather calm, protected by the strong walls on the ground floor.

When morning came they saw the widespread damage and realized how great a danger they had been in. All the windows of the church and convent were shattered. The window frames, door frames and doors were reduced to rubble. A main wall of the house had been penetrated by a howitzer shell, which had landed in the roomful of beds used by the young students, which was nothing but a mass of twisted iron. Everywhere they looked there were marks on the ceiling, chunks taken out of the walls, and holes in the eaves.[83]

Late in the morning of 17 June some cannon shells fired by the retreating German troops (who, it was said, were firing from Colcaprile and the hills of San Fortunato because they heard the bells in Assisi tolling in celebration and they saw the Italian flag flying above the Hotel Savoia) struck the Abbey of San Pietro and the monastery of the French Colettine nuns.[84] Some shells even grazed the dome of Santa Maria degli Angeli.

At the Porta San Giacomo two people were killed[85] and several were wounded. Several pieces of shrapnel fell near

---

83   Archives of the Protoconvento at Rivotorto.

84   Archives of the monastery of the Sisters of St. Colette, ms.

85   Roberto Raggi, a native of Eboli in the province of Salerno, who was a refugee in Assisi, and Francesco Chiarini, of San Giacomo (cf. Notiziario Assisano, 18 June 1994, p. 1).

Porta San Francesco, seriously wounding a young man from Assisi who was returning to Perugia, where he worked as a fire fighter and a 15-year-old boy, who died a short time later.[86]

Concerning the events of those two eventful days, we read in the chronicles of the Capuchin Convent in Assisi:

> 16 June: This evening was infernal. It seemed as if the end of the world had come. Fire was consuming everything. The retreating Germans gave vent to their anger, setting fire to everything and ruining even more than they could. The whole plain around Assisi was alight with the dancing of the flames. Mills, silos, body shops, all types of storage areas were set afire. Bridges, stations and villas were blown apart. Large numbers of animals had been taken from their owners and carried off....

> 17 June: With the retreat of the Germans and all the devastation which they willingly and knowingly inflicted upon us poor Italians whom they called traitors, this morning at 9:30 the English entered the piazza of the city on a few armored cars. They were greeted by the festive tolling of bells and an immense crowd of people. The city was immediately arrayed in British and American flags, and everyone strove to

---

86 The fireman was Leonello Costantini, who was taken to the hospital where, after a long agony and terrible suffering—and in part due to a lack of medicine—he died on 2 July, leaving a wife and three young children. He was 35 years old. The boy was Giuseppe Piantoni, known to all as "Peppino." Some of the shells hit the road where the Allied troops were passing. In that barrage a British soldier was also killed, and was given a hasty burial alongside the road. (Information furnished by Bruno Calzolari).

The first Allied troops enter the Piazza del Comune, morning of 17 June 1944.

celebrate our new bosses, our liberators. After discourses by various dignitaries, the English left the city, stopping for a brief time at the piazza San Francesco.

This great celebration was followed immediately by another fright. The Germans had taken up positions in the surrounding hills and seen the British enter the city which they had not been allowed to enter since it was a hospital city, and completely demilitarized. Therefore they began to fire upon the city.[87]

That very same day the local National Liberation Committee posted notices on all the walls of the city and the surrounding towns calling for a moral and spiritual rebirth in Italy.[88]

---

87   Archives of the Capuchin Convent in Assisi, *Cronaca del Convento*, written by Fr. Alberto of Gubbio.

88   Editor's note: They had survived one danger, but a new danger now arose: the establishment of armed Allied troops in the city could have provoked German air raids.
Bishop Nicolini continued his appeals to the Vatican and the Allied commanders over the next several months, so that neither armed troops nor their commanders nor any military supplies would be brought into the city.

THE TRUE STORY[1]

Aldo Brunacci

The book by Professor Francesco Santucci—*Assisi 1943-44 Documenti Per Una Storia*—published under the auspices of the *Accademia Properziana del Subasio* in 1994 on the occasion of the 50th anniversary of the city's liberation, has aroused great interest not only in Italy, but in other countries as well. This is to be expected, given the city's renown throughout the world and the truly heroic role its citizens played in 1943-1944 on behalf of several thousand refugees—including several hundred Jews as well as political refugees—all of whom came to the city of St. Francis confident of finding safety there.

At the end of the German occupation, 17 June 1944, all the refugees were able to return to their own homes, including many Jews, each of whom expressed gratitude to the Bishop of Assisi. Among the testimonials that Santucci includes in his appendix, page 136, is one by Prof. Emilio Viterbi, a scientist and dean at the University of Padua, who, together with his wife and two daughters, were lovingly welcomed and helped in Assisi.

---

1   By Don Aldo Brunacci. Previously published in *The Strategy That Saved Assisi*, Editrice Minerva Assisi 2000, pp. 67-78, this article was reworked for this edition. Used with permission.

On 15 May 1944, when the notorious Prefect Rocchi of Perugia sent police to arrest me, Emilio Viterbi and his wife were waiting for me in my office on Via San Francesco, because they no longer felt safe in their home and were in search of some other place of refuge. Fortunately the soldiers were not aware of their presence, because I closed the door behind me as I was led away.

In their confusion they knew to whom they could appeal. Prof. Viterbi writes:

> During the last period of the occupation the episcopal palace of Bishop Nicolini had become an asylum for a great number of refugees and persons who were being persecuted. Nonetheless, when I went to him to ask if, in the case of extreme difficulty, he could house me and my family, with great simplicity and a gentle smile, he said: 'There is no room left except my bedroom and my office. However, I can sleep in my office. The bedroom is yours.' This is what this distinguished prelate of Assisi was like.

Professor Santucci is the person with the best knowledge of Assisi's history today, for which reason he has been entrusted with the task of caring for the valuable archives of the Cathedral and Chancery. He has painstakingly examined all the documents of the many archives in the city and has succeeded in giving us a thorough view of this historical period, showing how much was being done for the liberation of Assisi.

Nor could I fail to add my observations, since at that time I was Bishop Nicolini's only collaborator and the secretary of the diocesan hospitality center at the Bishop's residence. To this center came refugees from cities that had been bombarded, Jews, and even many of Assisi's young people who spent their nights in the areas near the Bishop's house to avoid the German soldiers' nighttime military exercises.

Don Aldo Brunacci (1914 - 2007)

Even before Prof. Santucci, Francesco Salvatore Attal, a Jew who converted to Catholicism, published an article entitled *Assisi Città Santa Come Fu Salvata dagli Orrori della Guerra (Assisi: The Holy City and How It Was Preserved from the Horrors of War)*[2]. The author reports primarily on the letter-writing campaign between the religious and civil authorities, especially the Custos of the Sacro Convento, to protect the Basilica of St. Francis. However, in my opinion, he was not well-informed about the whole complex period

---

2   Miscellanea Francescana, periodical of the theological faculty of the Conventual Friars in Rome (volume 48, 1948, fasc. I, pp. 132).

under consideration.

Santucci also calls one of his chapters "Protecting the Cultural Resources." He shows that from January 1943 onwards, this was of great concern to the Superintendent of Medieval and Modern Art, Mr. Achille Bertini Calosso. In this regard Santucci mentions appeals to the warring parties made by the Minister of the Friars Minor Conventual, Fr. Bede Hess, an American citizen; by the Custos of the Sacro Convento, Fr Bonaventura Manzi; by the Bishop of Assisi, Placido Nicolini; and by the former Mayor of Assisi, Arnaldo Fortini, who also appealed to Mussolini—leader of the Republic of Salò by that time and having no real authority.

Santucci recounted this in order to be historically accurate, but in the end—and I, an eyewitness of what happened in Assisi at that time, could not be more in agreement with him—he had to state: "The city owed its salvation primarily to the fact that it had been proclaimed a hospital city." Thus it was not spared bombardment solely because of the invaluable artistic treasures it housed.

If that had been the real reason Assisi was saved, how could we explain the fact that the Abbey of Montecassino—of no less importance culturally and spiritually than the city of St. Francis—was destroyed. We must conclude that the two people most responsible for saving Assisi were Bishop Giuseppe Placido Nicolini, and Colonel Valentin Müller—a German officer—yes, an officer of Hitler's army.

Who was Valentin Müller? He was a medical officer, born in 1891 and died in 1951. In February 1944 this medical doctor was put in charge of the German hospitals in the city by the commanders of the German armed forces. The Colonel was a very religious man who attended daily mass and communion at the tomb of St. Francis.

With the Bishop's help, he realized that the only way to save the city would be to increase the number of hospitals in it so that it could be proclaimed a "hospital city." The Bishop worked closely with him in this matter. He was sure that this was the only way they could save the city of St. Francis, for whom Müller, as a Catholic, had a great love.

The front drew ever nearer and the number of the wounded grew. On 31 May—as I was told by the parish priest, Fr. Lamberto Petrucci—Colonel Müller and four other officers went to San Vitale where the Bishop was celebrating a parish feast. The Colonel asked the Bishop to grant him the use of the Pontifical Seminary of Umbria as a military hospital. The Bishop knew quite well that the seminary was the property of the Holy See, but because of the city's more compelling interest, he did not hesitate to grant the Colonel's request. As of that date, 31 May, the following buildings were used as hospitals:

— the Locatelli Palace (now Casa Papa Giovanni);

— the Seraphic Institute for the Blind and Deaf;

— the National Home for Orphans of Teachers;

— the Umbrian Regional Seminary.

On 5 June, following repeated requests, the friars of the Sacro Convento also decided to allow Colonel Müller to use the top floor of their Theological College as well. The warring parties recognized Assisi as a hospital city and for this reason it was respected.

Let me repeat that the two people most responsible for Assisi's safety were Bishop Nicolini and Colonel Müller. Müller's role was gratefully acknowledged by Assisi when it dedicated a street in his memory and installed a memorial plaque on Viale Vittorio Emanuele

Street in Assisi named after Dr. Valentin Müller

II, directly across from the Seraphic Institute, which was the first German military hospital in Assisi. Colonel Müller returned to Assisi during the Holy Year 1950, and was warmly welcomed by the entire city which had never forgotten him. When he left, he promised to return again. Several months later, however, he became ill and died soon after in his hometown.

In 1982, the eighth centenary of the birth of St. Francis, a delegation from Assisi went to Eichstätt to place olive branches from the hillsides of Assisi on Colonel Müller's grave. I had the honor of presiding at the prayers by his tomb and we were all moved to see carved on his tombstone the outline of the Basilica of St. Francis.

Bishop Nicolini's tomb is in the Chapel of the Pietà (to the left of the main altar) in the Cathedral of San Rufino. He died in the city of Trent, but the people of Assisi wanted him to return to the Church where he so frequently proclaimed the Gospel of peace. A bas-relief by Enrico Manfrini shows the Bishop with his mantle spread wide and children taking refuge under it. He was father of all the people during his episcopate in Assisi. However, in 1943/44 he was father as well of all those who took refuge in our city.

Before concluding this introduction, I feel it is my duty to point out that for the first time ever Prof. Santucci published a hand-written document of Bishop Nicolini: "The Story of the Medical Supplies." This refers to a great quantity of medicine and medical equipment that Colonel Müller, after the retreat of German troops, left behind in the city at great risk to himself. Unfortunately, a large part of this material was lost.

What Santucci is referring to is a direct communiqué from the chancery which I personally drafted at the time, following the Bishop's very clear instructions. This document also casts suspicion on the hero of the book, *Assisi Underground*, in which he was presented as Bishop Nicolini's collaborator. This lie was accepted most of all in America, to the point that in the Holocaust Memorial Museum in Washington, DC, in the entry under the name of Nicolini, we find Father Rufino Nicacci mentioned as his collaborator. No greater offense could have been given to a person like Bishop Placido Nicolini, who at great risk, saved so many Jews in Assisi.

Santucci's book does not go into the debate but simply presents the documentary evidence and renders justice against a book that has sold many copies as well as being made into a film.

In conclusion, I would like to join the President of the *Accademia Properziana del Subasio*, Prof. Giuseppe Catanzaro, in stating that the publication of such precious and unique documents will allow us to have precise knowledge of so many events and episodes of human solidarity. It will be evident to all how, in a period of passion and opposing views, a few citizens, some known to us and others forgotten, had overcome, even at great risk to their own persons, the divisions between ideologies and saw in each person a brother or sister whom they must save.

A PERSONAL NOTE
ON THE MEDICAL SUPPLIES

Bishop Nicolini[1]

This autograph of Bishop Nicolini is clear proof that Padre Rufino had no rapport with the Bishop. In this note the Bishop declares that he mistrusts (*Diffidato*) Padre Rufino: see Santucci, pp. 105-107.

Text as appears left:

"... *3. Ordine concertato col Comune.*

4. Opposizione di ditto Paolo... diffidato ripetutamente da me.
....

6. Diffidato anche P. Rufino, appena saputo del trasferimento. ..."

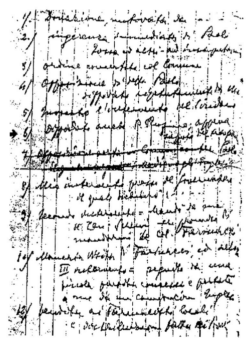

---

1   Bishop Nicolini's autograph from the diocesan archives. Used with permission.

Bishop Giuseppe Placido Nicolini, OSB (1877 – 1973)

THE UNSUNG HERO: BISHOP NICOLINI[1]

Aldo Brunacci

By way of several different publications I have tried to satisfy people's legitimate desire to know the truth about what was described by Alessandro Ramati in his book, *Assisi Clandestina* which was first published in Italian in 1982 by Porziuncola Press and was made into a film. (The English translation of the book was published under the title: *The Assisi Underground*.) It is truly a wonderful work of fiction, but pure fiction because it distorts the historical truth of a glorious period of Assisi's history, in which the main character of Ramati's book and film did not really play a leading role. I can state unequivocally that the true unsung hero of the period under discussion was Bishop Giuseppe Placido Nicolini, Bishop of Assisi at that time. I served as his sole comrade in this work, because the very nature of it required that he not take many into his confidence. On 5 January 1947, in an article entitled *The Heart of the Bishop During the War*, I wrote the following:

> Who is capable of writing the chronicle of such heroism, of such charity? Who could possibly describe the work of our pastor in this our Assisi

1   By Don Aldo Brunacci. First published in *The Strategy That Saved Assisi*, Editrice Minerva Assisi 2000, pp. 67-78. Editors' note: this article was reworked for this edition. Used with permission.

which, in fulfillment of St. Francis' prophecy, has never before been the refuge, the material and spiritual salvation of so many of the faithful as it was during this war? After the well-known events of July 1943 the Bishop's house became the single center of assistance for the many people who poured into the city from other cities under bombardment or from the front, which daily grew closer. That period saw the establishment of the Committee for Assistance, presided over by the Bishop, who continued his wide-reaching charitable activity until the end of the war. This committee, made up of diligent people, saw to the settlement of an immigrant population that at times equaled the population of the city. It created a center for the collection of essential items, especially of clothing, and a workshop was even established in the Bishop's residence.

Those who were fleeing persecution most of all found in Bishop Nicolini a shepherd with a Christ-like heart, and a welcome that could make them forget the hatred they were experiencing. In response to the Bishop's invitation, the convents and various religious communities took in about a hundred Jews and victims of persecution of every type. All this required a clandestine activity and a rather complex organization, which only a magnanimous person like Bishop Nicolini could have created.

The Bishop's kindness reached everywhere. Several times people who had just arrived and were waiting to be taken in somewhere else, or who were in imminent danger, were given refuge and a bed in the only room the Bishop had left. This great charitable activity never failed, despite the dangers, risks and threats of those who were watching over the work performed by the Bishop and myself. I will never forget how insistent those threats were, yet how determined the Bishop remained. He would not let anyone intimidate him from performing what he as pastor was required to do.

I recall very well the strength Bishop Nicolini showed in the face of the repeated alarms of the 'big shots' who felt it was their duty to suggest prudence and moderation. There are times in everyone's life in which it is easy to confuse prudence with a calm life. There are times when heroism is required. Bishop Nicolini took the path of heroism.

It is for this reason that when I was planning a pilgrimage to Jerusalem in December of 1977 and was invited to receive the medal and honors which the government of Israel reserves to those who worked to save Jews during World War II, I said that I was unable to accept this recognition unless it was first awarded to the person who was the true moving force behind this action. They replied that Bishop Nicolini had passed away. But I replied that the current Bishop of Assisi, as his successor, could receive the honor in his name.

The, ceremony took place on 11 December 1977, and was covered by the Israeli media. In a two-column article, the Jerusalem Post wrote: "The late Bishop of Assisi, Italy, who used the city's convents and monasteries to hide a hundred Jews during World War II, and his main collaborator, now Prior of the Cathedral of San Rufino in Assisi, will be honored in a ceremony at Yad Vashem in the Avenue of the Just. Representing the late Bishop will be his successor, Bishop. Dino Tommassini, who is in Israel conducting a pilgrimage.

Bishop Nicolini at home in Trento, 1973

Following the ceremony for the planting of a tree with a marker written in Hebrew and Italian, bearing the names of Bishop Giuseppe Placido Nicolini and Prof. Aldo Brunacci in the Park of the Just, an official reception was held in which Bishop Tommassini was given a certificate and medal in honor of Bishop Giuseppe Placido Nicolini, and I received the same. Each time that the speaker mentioned Bishop Nicolini's name, it was followed by the Biblical blessing, "may he be blessed forever."

I still have very many vivid memories of that time, and I would like to share some of them with you, dear readers. I am not always able to establish the exact date on which they occurred because prudence dictated that nothing should be written down.

One Thursday in September 1943, after the usual monthly meeting of the clergy in the diocesan seminary, the Bishop called me aside during a recess near the chapel and showed me a letter from the Vatican Secretariat of State and said to me: "We have to organize ourselves to help those who are being persecuted, especially the Jews. This is the desire of the Holy Father, Pope Pius XII. Everything must be done with the greatest secrecy and prudence. No one, not even the priests, must know anything about this."[2]

As I mentioned before, the Bishop's residence already hosted a center for aid to the refugees from areas afflicted by the war, and therefore it was not difficult to insert this new and sensitive action on behalf of the Jews into this vast organization. The Bishop's residence was spacious and had

---

2   In the book, *Pio XII, il privilegio di servirlo*, by Pascalina Lehnert (Rusconi Ed. 1984), one reads the following regarding the secret, and therefore efficacious work of Pius XII on behalf of the Jews:

"I recall in horror that morning in August 1942 when the newspaper headlines reported the horrible news that the official protest of the Dutch Bishops against the inhuman persecution of the Jews had led Hitler to take revenge by arresting 40,000 Jews that very night and sending them off to the gas chambers. The morning newspapers were brought to the Holy Father's study as he was getting ready for an audience. He only read the headlines, and turned pale. When he returned from his audience, it was already one o'clock, time for lunch, and before going to the dining room the Holy Father came into the kitchen (the only place it would have been possible to burn something unobserved), with two large pieces of paper covered with writing, and said: "I want to burn these papers. It is my protest against the terrible persecution of the Jews. It was supposed to be printed in L'Osservatore Romano this evening. But if the letter of the Dutch Bishops cost 40,000 human lives, my protest might cost 200,000. I cannot and must not take this responsibility. Therefore, it is better not to speak out officially and continue to do in silence everything humanly possible for these people" [pp. 148-149]. Two Dutch Jews escaped the retaliation and, after various vicissitudes, made their way to Assisi. Their name was Jacobson. I remember their inconsolable tears as they told me how the German soldiers led their two young sons, both in their twenties, away from home and they were never heard from again.

underground rooms. It was often necessary to hide, not only persons, but also the personal effects of those who were given refuge in the convents and private homes. There were precious objects, family mementos, and even objects and vestments for Jewish religious services, sacred texts—for there were some rabbis among the refugees—and all those items had to be kept in a place of greatest security.[3] These items were placed in recesses in the subterranean vault of the Bishop's residence and then walled over. The work was not done by workers, but by the Bishop himself who used the trowel to build the walls while I held the lantern. When a wall had to be broken into, I would wield the pick while the Bishop held the light for me. These operations were performed whenever we had to restore objects to individuals who were leaving Assisi even before the end of the war.

8 October 1943. The Jewish refugees in Assisi were celebrating their first Yom Kippur away from their homes, and for some of them, away from their homeland. I would like to quote what I wrote in an article for the *Catholic Times of London* on 19 August 1946:

> After the liberation the news about Assisi was reported with sensationalism by the foreign press For example, an English newspaper reported that

---

3   Editors' note: Did Colonel Müller have any idea about this? According to his son Robert: "If he was deceived, it was because he wanted to be deceived. If he had known, he would not have done anything to stop it. As a matter of fact, the house where he established his practice in Eichstätt had been purchased from a Jewish family. He paid for it in cash, allowing them to escape immediately. My father was also the last medical doctor to make visits to the homes of Jewish patients." Maximilian Schell, who portrayed Colonel Müller in the film version of Ramati's book, obviously depicted a very different character. From all that can be deduced, if Müller had known, he would not have acted differently.

the Jews in Assisi were able to have a synagogue in the crypt of the monastery founded by St. Francis. There is some truth in that article—that the Jews were absolutely free to gather for prayer in the quiet of the convents of Assisi—because it happened that, while the Sisters were intent on their prayer, under that same roof the Jews were invoking God's mercy and asking for peace and justice. On 8 December 1943 a group of various nationalities was gathered in the Monastery of San Quirico to celebrate the feast of Yom Kippur. The nuns had had the wonderful idea of decorating the dining room and the tables for a feast day. When the guests sat down to table to take their first meal after the feast and looked around, they no longer felt like strangers and they understood that in the bond of love they had been welcomed as brothers and sisters. I recall what a day of intense emotion that was!

9 November 1943. It was approximately seven o'clock in the morning. I was celebrating Mass at the Laboratorio San Francesco at the ancient Church of "Muro Rupto." During the celebration I was surprised to see Mrs. Krops from Trieste and her sister, Mrs. Maionica, waiting for me. At the end of Mass, amid their anguish they were able to tell me that the elderly Mrs. Weiss from Vienna, who had been suffering from cardiac problems for a few days, had died during the night, despite the care of Mrs. Maionica's doctor son. I had gone to visit her the previous day. Now we were faced with the problem of her burial. I hurried with them to San Quirico and, after saying a brief prayer over the body,

told the ladies I would take care of everything. No one at the city offices was surprised that an elderly refugee had died in Assisi. I explained that she had given me the money to buy a burial place in the cemetery in my name.

The "commission of the just" honors Bishop Nicolini on 11 December 1977

That same day, as dusk was beginning to fall, accompanied by very few people, we carried her to the cemetery. The evening was very cold. When we arrived at the cemetery we had the coffin placed, as usual, at the entrance of the chapel. I went to the custodian, Guerrino Lanfaloni, my elementary school classmate, and told him: "It is too cold to have the customary prayers here. We did everything at San Quirico. Let us take the coffin immediately into the mortuary and bury her tomorrow." On the tomb we placed an inscription naming "Bianca Bianchi," translating her surname into its Italian equivalent. It remained like this until war's end. As we silently proceeded along the road towards the cemetery, we ran into a German patrol whose members immediately stood at attention, never knowing that the coffin they saluted contained the body of a Jewish lady. At the end of the war Mrs. Weiss' son came to visit. He had taken refuge in Brazil. I went with him to his mother's tomb, and together we made arrangements to have the stone changed. Today the tomb of Mrs. Weiss can still be found in the cemetery of Assisi, with the Star of David above this inscription: KERFA FELD CLARA, widow WEISS, born at Vienna on 15 September 1887 and died peacefully in Assisi, where she had found loving hospitality during the Nazi persecution, on 9 November 1943.

I have many memories of that time that I could share with you, some of them happy and some not so happy. However, I would also like to mention some of those who worked with me in helping our Jewish brothers and sisters, and who are no longer among the living. First in chronological order was the Conventual, Fr. Michele Todde, from the Basilica of St. Francis. It was he who sent us the first group of Jews, who were then lodged in San Quirico. The Church of St. Francis was a natural place for those who came to Assisi seeking help. Fr. Todde knew all the places in which we were hiding people, and which we continually changed, for obvious reasons: the Laboratorio San Francesco, the Convent of the German Sisters, the Cathedral and the Diocesan Seminary.

Fr. Rufino Nicacci, OFM, in his role as guardian of San Damiano, often went to San Quirico. Thus he befriended the first group that was given refuge there, and he joined our clandestine organization, offering courageous assistance because of this courageous enterprise. Fr. Federico Vincenti, was parish priest of Sant' Andrea in Perugia, whose parish was another point of reference. A group of young Jews lived in the attic of his home. I also slept in this attic when I went to Perugia by bicycle on sensitive missions at dusk. In the morning I would go back to Assisi by bicycle, joining up with the German transports along the road so as not to be late for school. Bishop Minestrini, prison chaplain in Perugia, offered invaluable help when a group of young Jews was arrested. He also helped me after that fateful 15 May when I was imprisoned by the police, by order of the notorious Prefect Rocchi.

Among the many Jews, I feel it is my duty to make special mention of Giorgio Krops, who was my good friend until his tragic death in Trieste in 1963. After he had spent some time in Assisi, this protected person became the protector of others; the saved person became the savior of others. Because of his quick intellect, he became the heart and soul of the group of Jews, together with two officers who were also in hiding at San Quirico: Colonel Gay, an Official of the High Command of the Italian Military, and Lieutenant Pilota Podda. This group worked on behalf of those who were being persecuted, especially the needy. It was they who organized the printing of the false identity cards. They continued working until the early days of May 1944, when some of them were arrested in Perugia. I cannot give first-hand evidence of anything that happened after 15 May 1944, because on that day I was also arrested. Let me to add something about that event.

It was evening, and I was returning home from the May devotions in the Church of Santo Stefano. I was met at the door of my house by two policemen in civilian dress who told me that they had orders from Prefect Rocchi to take me to Perugia. I asked them if I could please go into the house to get some things and my breviary. In my study I found Emilio and Margherita Viterbi,[4] a Jewish couple from Padua who, completely ignorant of the events happening to me, were waiting for me to come home to ask if I could please find them a new refuge because they no longer felt safe where they were staying. I told them not to move. I took my breviary and I closed the door after me, said good-bye to my parents and went off with the policemen. After ten days of confinement and a ridiculous trial based on some vague accusations I was allowed to take refuge in the Vatican, where I remained until a few days after Assisi's liberation.

Earlier I mentioned a Jew who died. I would also like to make mention of two people who were born. Maria-Enrico Finzi was born in the convent of the French Colettine Poor Clares shortly after the liberation. This family—father, mother and a three-year-old daughter—came from Belgium and were already in Assisi on 8 September 1943, so the birth of the new child was regularly reported to the police with the child's true name.

After 8 September they had been stopped several times and, in order to save them, Bishop Nicolini gave permission for the whole family to enter the cloister in Santa Coletta. That monastery had the most rigid enclosure of all the monasteries in Assisi. The Abbess at that time was Mother Helene, an exceptional woman, who had her degree from

---

4   The well-known Prof. Emilio Viterbi, a scientist at the University of Padua, together with his wife Margherita Levi Minzi and his daughters Grazia Benvenuta and Mirjam Rosa, had come to Assisi in October 1943.

the Sorbonne. We were good friends and held each other in high esteem. For some time I had also been her confessor, but I never saw her face.

In fact, even when we met in the parlor we were separated by two grilles, behind which she frequently wore a black veil over her face. Yet with the Bishop's permission, Mother Helene let the Finzi family into the cloister. The little family lived in a single room at the end of a corridor, and little Brigitte had free range to run back and forth among the choir sisters in their work room, kitchen and chapter room. In 1964, twenty years after the little girl's birth, the monastery of the Colettine Poor Clares received a notice that M. Enrico Finzi must report for military service. However, the family had returned to Belgium after the war.

Bas-relief on the tomb of Bishop Nicolini (†1973), Cathedral San Rufino, Assisi

The other new baby was Francesco Clerici. He was not Jewish, but was the son of a navy officer who was in hiding in the guest house of the German Sisters of the Holy Cross where other Jews were also hidden. Officer Clerici served as our contact person in this monastery, and helped us settle in new refugees when they arrived.

For some time the Jewish writer Dino Provenzal—also sent to me by Fr. Todde—was given refuge in the monastery of the German sisters. His forged documents listed his name as Pastore, and with this name his children and the children of other Jews with false documents, attended school regularly. After the war they had their records changed.

I could continue forever, reminiscing about this period when people worked side by side for the single ideal of freedom. People of different ideas, religions, race and nationalities together imagined a bright future. We too must be heralds of peace, fighting with the same enthusiasm and faith of yesterday for fraternity among all peoples and the banishment of every type of racial or religious discrimination. This is the message we want to hand on to future generations and the whole world. Jews and Christians venerate the same book, the Bible, whose opening chapter reminds us that we are created in God's image and likeness. God is our Father, and we are all brothers and sisters.

ASSISI HERO:
RESPECTED BY CHRISTIANS AND JEWS[1]

Susan Saint Sing

Dinner at Casa Papa Giovanni begins promptly at 7:30. I have 15 minutes. It is late August and Assisi is uncharacteristically cool for this time of year. The streets are jammed with tourists who chose not to go to the beach for the August holidays but to visit Assisi and other hill towns in the region.

I am happy when I step into the relative solitude of the cool, travertine hallway of the Casa and the four-inch-thick, 10-foot-high door closes behind me. With only minutes to spare, I take the marble steps of the staircase two at a time to wash up before the evening meal. Memories from 20 years ago, when I first met our host, Don Aldo Brunacci, flash through my mind.

MEETING AND MIRACLE

It is the summer of 1977, a cool morning in Assisi. Don Aldo is crossing the shaded central piazza to say Mass at the Cathedral of San Rufino. I am crossing in the opposite direction to visit the Basilica of St. Francis. I recall the morning mist burning off the plain below and the distant

---

1   By Susan Saint Sing in: St. Anthony Messenger, USA, February 1999. Used with permission.

dome of St. Mary of the Angels shining gold against the blue Umbrian sky.

As I enter the piazza, Don Aldo and I are introduced by a third man, an Australian friar named Father Thaddeus (now deceased), who is having his morning cappuccino. He jumps up from his seat at the Bar Minerva and, sidestepping the pigeons, creates an introduction that will frame the rest of my life.

He explains to Don Aldo that I am a student from America looking for work in Assisi for room-and-board in a *pensione*. Father Thaddeus then turns to me and says: "Susan, this is Don Aldo, a Canon of the Cathedral of San Rufino and the head of Casa Papa Giovanni, a major retreat house in Assisi."

Don Aldo's response stuns me. "Yes, you can come and work with us at the Casa."

A friend of mine had told me that Assisi was a magical city, so I unhesitatingly accept his offer as a miracle. After all, this is Assisi! Of course, I would find a job quickly. Nor does it seem extraordinary that I am treated as one of the family at Casa Papa Giovanni, that Don Aldo becomes a close friend who muses over my journal of drawings and fragments of poems written in Italian. He guides me on walking tours through the fields of Monte Subasio to places where he feels the true caves of St. Francis are to be found.

Don Aldo frequently tries to get me to explain to him and the Bishop of Assisi (who lives in the house) about the Church in the United States and why a twenty-two-year-old collegian would want to give up her life in the U.S. and come to Assisi.

I eventually share the story of my father's recent death, and the severe neck and back injury that brought me to Assisi to seek healing.

'WHOEVER SAVES A SINGLE SOUL...'

Tonight, I suspect it was better that I didn't know 20 years back how great a contribution Don Aldo Brunacci has made to Assisi and the world. I now know that he was a key figure in Assisi's World War II history, the esteemed prior of the Canons of the Cathedral of San Rufino and dean of judges for the regional matrimonial tribunal.

The very year of our first meeting, on December 11, he was awarded the Medal of the Righteous Gentile from the State of Israel for his part in helping to save Jewish refugees. A Righteous Gentile is a non-Jew who risked his or her life to help save Jews. The medal Don Aldo shows his dinner guests is from the Yad Vashem Museum and Research Center in Israel and has been bestowed on more than 11,000 rescuers. He is also recognized for this action in the Holocaust Museum in Washington, D.C.

The award ceremony is a public and solemn occasion. In her book *Conscience and Courage*, historian Eva Fogelman explains: "A carob tree is planted along the Avenue of the Righteous, an avenue that leads to the museum itself, and a plaque bearing the rescuer's name and nationality marks the tree. The story of the rescuer's deed is recounted at the ceremony and filed in the museum's archives. Israeli officials then present the rescuer, or in some cases an entire rescuing group, with a medal and a certificate. The medal bears a Talmudic inscription: 'Whoever saves a single soul, it is as if he had saved the whole world.'"

One such survivor, Graziella Viterbi, still lives in Assisi. Hers was one of the Jewish families Don Aldo helped hide and relocate in Assisi. She was, in fact, in Don Aldo's house when two policemen were sent by Prefect Rocchi to arrest him. She thanks God to this day that they did not search his residence.

I ask this modest man for details of these years of war and holocaust. Don Aldo keeps them always in his heart.

PEACEFUL ASSISI IN A TIME OF PERIL

The Jews began to arrive in Assisi in September 1943, just after the German occupation. Many came from the north. Don Aldo recalls: "Our first concern was to get them safely lodged in the various monasteries and convents or with reliable families who would 'forget' to comply with the police regulations to denounce any strangers in their houses. The chief center was the convent of San Quirico, where the Jewish refugees were generally housed until we could provide them with new ration books and all the papers they needed to live unmolested."

"The printing of the documents and especially the procuring of the official stamps was a difficult and risky job. All their real personal documents, as well as their sacred books and religious objects, were hidden in the cellars of the palace of the Bishop of Assisi," says the priest.

Don Aldo praises Colonel Valentin Müller, the German commandant of the occupied city of Assisi. He was a devout Catholic, devoted to St. Francis from childhood, a sympathetic man through whom Bishop Nicolini ceded to the German Medical Command many of the religious buildings in and around Assisi for the establishment of hospitals.

Don Aldo himself was arrested on May 15, 1944, and was due to be sent to a concentration camp. But on June 4, the Allies entered Rome. Don Aldo and the others imprisoned were liberated. And of course, by then the underground was no longer needed.

PUTTING HISTORY RIGHT

When asked about popular films and books on this aspect of Assisi's history, Don Aldo becomes quite animated about the truth of the Holocaust. He cares nothing about recognition but, because he put his own life in harm's way to help, he has a right to see that the story gets straightened out.

The Assisi Underground, the most famous of the accounts of this period, is a dramatic fiction which places a friar in the key position. The author, Alexander Ramati, was anticipating a feature film, according to Don Aldo. But Don Aldo was there and he remembers the story somewhat differently: "The truth about the events which took place in Assisi is much more interesting than the coarse, unlikely and romanticized story which unfortunately was taken as truth...."

In addition to his own remembrance, Don Aldo has documents stating that the unheralded Bishop of Assisi, Giuseppe Placido Nicolini, at the time of the war, "was the impetus, inspiration, fortitude and ecclesiastical savvy behind housing, feeding, hiding, schooling, preparing false papers for and aiding the escape of some 200 Jews hidden in the homes and monasteries of Assisi." In a parallel action, Archbishop Angelo Roncalli—later to become known as Pope John XXIII—was changing birth certificates of Jews to "Catholic," securing safe passage for them out of Italy.

Why did so many Jews choose Assisi as a refuge in 1943? Don Aldo explains: "They felt drawn there by St. Francis. When the danger had passed, many told me that they attributed their safety to him."

Don Aldo becomes almost agitated and disappears into his office. He surfaces with photographs, letters and sworn documents proving that only a Bishop, not the Padre Rufino of the romanticized book-turned-film under the American title *The Assisi Underground*, could hoodwink the Nazis and pull off such a complicated, covert operation.

In the film, the Franciscan friars are given more credit for the safety of the Jews in Assisi than they were in a position to provide. It's a laughable fiction, really, since even St. Francis put himself under the local Bishop. Nothing of such magnitude could have occurred in Assisi without the Bishop spearheading it. It distresses Don Aldo, as evidenced by his direct words, that this distortion of facts—a simple friar championing the entire operation—has gained credibility and is widely accepted as true.

On June 23, 1978, Dr. Denise Pilkington of the European Editorial Office of *Reader's Digest* wrote to Don Aldo after visiting Assisi for several days to research the story of the then-newly released book describing Padre Rufino's heroism: "You will not be surprised to learn that we shall not publish that book! Because only history is worth telling."

It becomes clear to me that Don Aldo is having this candid conversation for my benefit. I understand the gravity of the issue and appreciate the quiet, organized way in which real heroes saved lives.

SON OF ST. FRANCIS

Perhaps Don Aldo's rescue of Jews during the war is one reason that, behind the closed doors and walled streets of Assisi's cobblestone walks and gated houses, Don Aldo is sought out for his wisdom by families, artisans, business people and politicians.

The swarms of tourists, who come to the medieval town in hope of some spiritual solace amid the kitsch of Italian shopkeepers' glow-in-the-dark "Francescoes" on a sultry August afternoon, seldom see this priest. He passes unnoticed, as he prefers, calmly doing his work for Church and city and St. Francis in his own unassuming, scholarly, accurate way.

Now 84 years old, soled in black sandals, wearing black pants, usually a pale blue polyester shirt and black suit coat, he smiles easily looking over his bifocals, spryly dodging UPS trucks, as he makes his way daily between his bookshop and press, *Libreria Fonteviva*, and the Cathedral of San Rufino.

I think back to a rare evening stroll with Don Aldo and other friends. As we made our way to a concert in the town hall, progress was halting as local Assisians deferred to Don Aldo's passing, "Good evening, Don Aldo."

Babies were held for him to look at, fathers strode across the piazza to intercept him (as I now realize Father Thaddeus had done 20 years earlier on my behalf) to get some private moment or answer in a quick flurry of Italian. Groups of pilgrims, everywhere in the festive streets, sometimes stopped and heads turned as guides clandestinely pointed out Don Aldo in the crowd.

I felt humble and patiently waited to the side as people jogged his memory about events of the past or appointments for the future he was to attend. "Si, si, si, si" was his standard four-syllable response. I had heard it often in our 20-year friendship.

This evening meal is two weeks before the September 1997 earthquake. During the first course of pasta and broth, green salad and bread, we dinner guests discuss politics, ostrich farms, olive trees and at rare intervals—Don Aldo himself. My mind juxtaposes the dinners from past and present and I smile. Conversation flows easily.

Don Aldo is every bit an Assisian. He was born in Assisi on April 2, 1914. His elementary schooling was in the Palazzo Locatelli, which is today the very Casa Papa Giovanni where we now dine.

Casa Papa Giovanni means *House of Pope John* and is so named for Pope John XXIII. Don Aldo speaks of Pope John and the Second Vatican Council during which the Casa's bookstore, *Libreria Fonteviva*, was founded and after which the Casa itself was donated as a religious foundation by the Diocese of Assisi.

He tells of the Church and the history of St. Francis. He recalls his appointment to travel to Baltimore to examine for authenticity a liturgical missal thought to be the actual missal once opened by St. Francis for guidance.

Don Aldo speaks of changing times as a local, as one born and raised here: how dear the houses and the land are to buy, and how Assisi has become so replete with shops and souvenirs that he welcomes people now, tongue in cheek, to the town of Francis' merchant father, Pietro Bernardone, instead of Francesco Bernardone himself.

Don Aldo goes on to talk about how Assisi through the ages has been the spinal cord of strategic military importance with travel up and down the axis of Italy, from Roman legions to Napoleon in 1797-1798 housing his army's horses in the Basilica of St. Mary of the Angels and deporting the Bishop of Assisi and some of the parish priests to France! I am reminded that Don Aldo Brunacci is not only a part of history but a scholar of history in his own right. He is a Latin and Greek classicist, who brings his immense classical learning to his understanding of Assisi's and Italy's history.

He worries about the *Casa*, an institute of religious hospitality, a center of Franciscan study and retreat with its library, classroom, chapel, elevator, roof garden, olive trees, roses, zinnias, balconies constructed trellis-like up the hillside with porticoes of travertine and ceilings of Renaissance frescoes. The rooms for pilgrims cover three floors and are surprisingly spartan: a cell, with a modest desk, bed and chair.

The views of Perugia, the plain, the fortress above the city and the serenity in the roof garden are cuddled beneath terra cotta roof tiles and cool plaster walls. It is an oasis in the Umbrian heat, above the racket of the constant flow of walkers-by, delivery trucks and horns on Via San Paolo.

The hour grows late and Assisi's bells peal under the black sky and etched stars. A modern troubadour's guitar-strums, accompanied by six or seven voices, reverberate through the courtyard. Don Aldo remembers, "When I was a young cleric, I rode my bike everywhere throughout the diocese. All through the countryside the farmers would be singing, too, and working to the songs. Different songs for different work." He says: "Assisi has always been a place where people feel free to sing."

I ask Don Aldo what he wishes to see in the next millennium. He says without hesitation, "Peace." He is indeed the servant of St. Francis. He is a churchman of honor and rank, equivalent to a monsignor, yet he wears no red, drives his own car, walks about town, assumes no airs. He speaks of peace as a man who has lived through war, as a man who was imprisoned for his part in aiding Jews and refugees in Assisi during the war.

As dinner comes to a close, with the table strewn with pages of files and news clippings, photos from Israel, linen napkins, vino, cameras and quiet glances sealed in nods, hugs and hushed Italian, I know that this evening is about to end.

We have been talking since 7:30 p.m. and it is now nearly 11. As we walk through the roof garden gate and turn to face the hill's night coolness sweetened by ginestra, we silently muse over the complex recollections Don Aldo has just shared with us.

I am rapt in the magic of Assisi: a tapestry from ancient Rome to the Middle Ages to the present, artfully woven by a true troubadour and son of St. Francis, Don Aldo Brunacci.

IN ASSISI
NOT ONE WAS TOUCHED[1]

Aldo Brunacci

Who can possibly write the account of such charity in our city, Assisi? According to the prophecy of St. Francis, Assisi has never before been refuge and salvation, both physical and spiritual, for so many people as it was during this conflict.

We must remember two important dates: July 25, 1943, which saw the fall of the Fascist regime, and September 8, 1943, the day when the government broke off its alliance with Hitler and took sides with the Allied forces.

In retaliation for this affront the Germans occupied central and northern Italy, including Rome and Assisi. Only the most fanatical Fascists sided with them, becoming very dangerous spies. As a result, the Bishop's residence became the only center of assistance for those who were flowing into Assisi to escape both from the cities that were being bombed and from the war front, which was getting closer every day. It was then that the assistance committee, headed by the Bishop, came into existence; it continued until the

---

[1]   *Italian Priest Remembers Holocaust Heroism* in: Jewish Standard, June 7, 2002. Used with permission.
Editors's note: On April 26, Don Aldo Brunacci spoke at Temple Emanuel of the Pascack Valley in Woodcliff Lake. These are edited excerpts from his talk.

end of the war. This committee sheltered an immigrant population that at one point was as large as the population of Assisi itself.

Some Jewish families had arrived in Assisi even before September 8 but after this date, even more arrived. One day that month, the Bishop called me aside and said: "We must get organized to help those who are persecuted and above all the Jews. All must be done with the utmost discretion and reserve. No one, not even the clergy, must know about this."

With the Bishop's help, a center where refugees arrived from war-devastated countries had already opened. It was not difficult to work within that large organization to help Jews. The Bishop's residence in Assisi is large, with sizeable cellars. Often both people and their belongings had to be hidden. There were things that were inherently valuable and others that held precious memories. These special objects were hidden in the cellars, and the cellars were walled off. This task was not to be entrusted to regular bricklayers, so it was the Bishop himself who took trowel in hand while I held a candle so we could see. When there was digging to be done we changed places; I dug and he held the candle. When people had to leave before the war's end, the work had to be undone, their belongings removed, and the cellar re-sealed.

After September 8, more Jews arrived. Their numbers swelled again after the German occupation was firmly consolidated. They came from Trieste, Padua, Milan, France, Austria, and Yugoslavia. Although the Bishop's residence was our organization's headquarters, the refugees were placed in the Convent of San Quirico and in the guest rooms of Santa Croce, the German Capuchin Sisters' convent. They remained there until they were given false identity cards, which were necessary because without them the refugees could not receive ration cards to obtain food. With these new papers, our guests were able to live undisturbed, even in hotels or private apartments.

Printing the documents was a difficult and risky job. It was even harder and more risky to make the rubber stamps. Among the people who helped us was a firmly anti-Fascist typographer who had a small, pedal-driven printing press (presently part of the exhibition, "Museum of Memory: Assisi 1943-44," at the Vallemani Palace on the Via San Francesco).

Pedal-powered printing press used by Trento and Luigi Brizi to produce false identity cards.

Even with false identity cards, people still had to be very careful. One young lady, who according to her false identity card was from Bari, but answered her questioners with a Venetian accent. Her presence of mind, combined with the instructions she had been given, saved her when she insisted that she picked up the accent because she studied in Venice.

One evening, a man of Polish descent who had always lived in France, his wife, and their children arrived in Assisi; they'd escaped from a French concentration camp and crossed the Alps on foot. None of them spoke Italian. The diocese of Genoa sent them to Florence and then on to Assisi. The secretary of the Archbishop of Genoa gave them false papers that said they were Italians returning from French-speaking Tunisia. We found shelter for them with the French Poor Clares until they received their ration cards, and we hid them in a small apartment above a hayloft reachable only by ladder.

A Russian family was housed in the convent and so was a Belgian family named Finzi. The Finzis arrived in Assisi before the Germans occupied it, so they had been registered. Therefore, the police came to get them, but they were not at home. The convent's abbess immediately got the Bishop's permission to hide the family in the cloister, a place so sacred the police did not dare violate it. After the liberation, a baby, Enrico Finzi, was born in the convent.

An elderly Viennese lady died in the convent of San Quirico. The other refugees fretted over her burial. "Don't worry," I said to them, "I'll take care of everything without raising the least suspicion." I went to the municipal authorities and bought a burial niche. I told them it was for a refugee who had left me money to do so. I escorted the coffin to the cemetery, and a German patrol passed by respectfully, never guessing that under the funeral pall was a Jew. She was buried as Bianca Bianchi, the name she'd been using in Assisi. After liberation, her son, who had gone to Brazil, came to find her grave. We put her real name, along with a star of David, on a new tombstone.

We incurred many dangers and had to move refugees constantly because we were afraid our neighbors were getting suspicious. Some pastors helped us find new hiding places. Father Federico Vincenti hid some young Jewish men in Perugia. Sometimes I would sleep in the refugees' shelters. I would leave Assisi at sundown by bicycle and ride back in time for school. If it was late, I would hold on to the back of a German military transport truck.

One day the police came to my door, just when Prof. Emilio Viterbi and his wife, Margherita, Jews from Padua, were in my study. They wanted me to find them a new, safer place to live. I reassured the Viterbis, closed the study door, said goodbye to my parents, and went with the police, who did not search my parents' house. I was confined in a makeshift concentration camp in Perugia, and told that my fate would be decided by Prefect Rocchi, a Fascist leader who collaborated with the Germans. Fortunately, by that time the Allies were just outside Rome, which was liberated on June 4. I was able to escape to Rome and find shelter in the Vatican.

When the Jews were in Assisi I developed a real, fraternal friendship with them, their faith, and their culture, based on mutual esteem and respect. I shall never forget the deep emotion I felt on October 8, 1943, when a large group of Jews of different nationalities gathered in a room in the convent to celebrate Yom Kippur. The nuns had decorated the refectory and the tables with flowers. When the guests sat down for the meal, the nuns decided to serve the meal that closed their own penitential day. The guests no longer felt like strangers; they looked one another in the eye and understood that they had been received as brothers and sisters.

At the end of the war, Dr. Renzo Levi, representing a group of refugees, wrote to Bishop Nicolini. His letter read:

> Even here in Rome, the ecclesiastical organizations were lavish in their help and advice, but the work of Your Excellency turned out to be particularly worthy of gratitude because we were happy to learn that not one of our refugees lost his life in Assisi, nor was there any deportation, as, unfortunately, was the case more than once here in Rome.

In a testimonial he delivered on January 6, 1946, for Bishop Nicolini's 70th birthday, Prof. Viterbi wrote: "We shall always tell our children and every one else...during a persecution that annihilated 6 million Jews...in Assisi not one was touched!"

May this be an example of the real brotherhood that should unite all humankind.

FROM A COURAGEOUS YOUTH
OF YESTERDAY
A TESTIMONY OF FAITH, HUMANITY,
AND PEACE FOR THE YOUTH OF TODAY[1]

Mario Spinelli

Occasionally, honors are bestowed on people or organizations merely for show, but who have accomplished nothing. However, recently that was not the case. For the authority standing behind the honor and the person receiving the recognition were outstanding. We are referring to The Day of Remembrance celebrated on January 27 in Italy to remember the persecution and extermination of the Jews in the Nazi concentration camps during World War II. On that occasion the President of the Italian Republic, Carlo Azeglio Ciampi officially conferred the honor of Knight of the Great Cross, upon Don Aldo Brunacci, a priest of Assisi, today a nonagenarian, for the support, assistance, and solidarity shown the refugees and persecuted Jews during the last tragic years of the war.

During those years of bloodshed and violence as the Germans and Anglo-Americans fought in Italy, people came forward in the name of human and Christian solidarity to protect and save many lives at great personal risk, regardless of

---

1   A Conversation in Assisi with Don Aldo Brunacci, originally published in L'Osservatore Romano, Feb. 8, 2003, p. 11, by Mario Spinelli. Used with permission.

faith or nationality. Among these courageous and generous benefactors was Don Aldo Brunacci, who worked together with Bishop Guiseppe Placido Nicolini, the Bishop of Assisi during those years. Whenever house searches were made, they hid hundreds of Jews, both Italian and foreign, thus saving them from deportation and certain death.

The festive occasion of this high honor gave Don Aldo a chance to take another and deeper look at the events of those tragic and courageous years.

Between 1943-1945 the Italian Church—its bishops, priests, religious, lay people, convents and Catholic organizations— was first in line to offer aid to all those suffering, and at great risk because of this brutal conflict. It was an historical event now recognized by all. The award of Knight of the Great Cross, given to Don Aldo Brunacci by the Italian government, is an acknowledgment, on behalf of the Italian people, of the role of the Church for the risks taken during these years of war and bloodshed.

We spoke about these and other matters with Don Aldo (still youthful and full of vigor despite his advanced age) in his native Assisi, in the Bishop's house, the very scene of many dramatic acts of heroism on his part and that of Bishop Nicolini. Don Aldo's reactions, answers, and reflections fully reveal him in all his simplicity, modesty, humility, but full of candor. This elderly hero has preserved all the idealism and purity of his intrepid youth.

Beloved Don Brunacci, first of all let's speak of the effect upon you of receiving such a high honor from the first citizen of your country.

Truthfully, I've only received a telegram from the General Secretary of the President of the Republic, telling me of the honor to be conferred on me. At the present time I don't know when the celebration will take place. Certainly I'm a little surprised and pleased at the same time. Indeed, the message from the ministry did not specify the reasons, and at the beginning I was uncertain why I was being honored. I thought that perhaps someone was pulling my leg. But still, I am pleased, remembering all the time that has passed by—now sixty years.

What recollections do you have of those events?

I remember the events very well. I was young, thirty years of age. The images are permanently stamped on my mind. It was a very hectic period. And it's a good thing that we are having this interview here in the Bishop's house, for Bishop Nicolini was the heart and center of all the activities for assistance and aid. After July 25, 1943 it had fallen to him to take control of so many civic responsibilities, since the civil authorities had abandoned ship. In the Bishop's house a large committee was established. The Bishop was its president, and I was its secretary.

More than 4,000 refugees came to Assisi from cities bombed in southern Italy, and we tried to arrange things for them the best we could. But after September 8 we added the work of assisting those being persecuted by the government, especially the Jews. One day Bishop Nicolini showed me a letter from the Secretary of State in which the Vatican recommended that we give maximum assistance to those who were being persecuted, above all to the Jews. When the Jewish families began to arrive in large numbers, we first turned to the Basilica of San Francesco and to the Sacro Convento, which were the natural places to go.

So you collaborated with the Franciscan friars?

I remember the sacristan, Father Todde, who sent me some Jewish refugee families who needed care. But the Sacro Convento was too obvious a hiding place. So they hid the Jewish families in the guest rooms of other friaries and monasteries—with the German Sisters, the Franciscan Colettine nuns, the Sisters of San Quirico, the Holy Cross Sisters, the Stigmatines and so many others. I also placed them with many private families, whom I trusted.

Furthermore, we provided the refugees with a new identity, giving them new names and documents, making them hail from a city in Italy where there weren't many Germans. A movie was made of these events, *Assisi Underground*, with Jews dressed as friars and other things of that sort. But it was a distortion of that page of history.

Where you afraid, Father? When was it the most risky?

From what I've already said and repeat every chance I get,

the one who deserves the credit for all these works is above all my Bishop at that time. The award of the Knight of the Great Cross should have been given in his memory. In 1977 when I was honored with the title of "The Just of Israel" and invited to Jerusalem to plant a tree in the Park of the Just, I said that I would accept only if they gave the same honor first of all to Bishop Nicolini. So I went to Jerusalem together with his successor, Bishop Dino Tomassini. Bishop Nicolini was declared one of "The Just of Israel." And Bishop Tomassini and I planted a memorial tree.

Your own modesty and your dedication to the memory of your Bishop bring honor to you, Don Aldo. But without your own courage and work, would the head of the diocese have had a voice and been able to perform his works of charity and solidarity? Weren't you the more visible and the more vulnerable diocesan worker?

Yes, that's true. I had no fear nor did I think of the risks involved. I thought only that I was fighting for a just cause and that was enough to give me courage and perseverance. I was only concerned about my parents, because in those months Assisi was full of spies for OVRA[2]. The Germans had other things to think about, and pressed into service Fascist collaborators and militia. One day Bishop Nicolini showed me a lot of photos—I don't know how he got them— in which I had been photographed talking with people in all sectors of Assisi. Clearly it was the work of OVRA. And

---

2   Editors' note: Don Aldo Brunacci remembers them as secret police.

in fact on May 15 of 1944 I found the police at my door.

And what happened?

They carted me off to Perugia to a makeshift and hostile tribunal, composed of collaborators and militia of the Republic of Salò. They accused me of ridiculous and incredible things. Since they could not touch the Bishop, they leveled all their attacks at me. They threatened to deport me to Germany, but there was no time, for the Allies were making great advances. They put me into a Perugian school that functioned as a concentration camp from which I managed to escape to Rome.

How many Jews did you save?

Since I never kept an exact count, I cannot answer your question with any precision. But between Assisi and its outlying areas, we estimate no less than 300.

One final question, Father. You saved so many Jews during World War II and were a Catholic priest. During these days there is criticism of Pope Pius XII that he didn't do enough for the persecuted and refugee Jews at the same time that you were doing so much, but kept a culpable silence. What's your thought about this matter?

I respond with a recent event. Last year I was in the USA, invited by two universities (St. Francis in Brooklyn, NY and St. Bonaventure in Olean, NY) and three synagogues. In Buffalo I met with the council of the Jewish community of that city. The television people were there and asked so many questions. Of course, one of the questions touched on the presumed silence of Pius XII.

I first answered with another question: Tell me, is it better to speak or to act? And after I got the response naturally, to act, I cited studies and documents which calculated that Pius XII saved from deportation and death at least 800,000 Jews. For the rest, I have already mentioned the letter from the Vatican Secretary of State, dated September 1943, asking Bishop Nicolini to protect the refugees and in particular the Jews. But there is more. There are entire volumes—the Jesuits have worked very much in this area—which demonstrate the solidarity and specific actions taken by Pope Pacelli in defense of the Jews persecuted by the Nazis.

JEWISH REFUGEES

Aldo Brunacci

In a recent edition of the CATHOLIC TIMES I noticed a paragraph about Jews in Assisi during the war. The details had been transmitted to the National Catholic Welfare Conference of America by the Rabbi R.E. Resnik, director in Italy of the Committee of American Assistance to the Jews. And as I was personally involved in the work of protecting these persecuted people, I thought it might be of interest to English readers to know how we carried out our efforts.

The Jews began to arrive in Assisi in September 1943, after the German occupation. Many of them came from the north and I often asked them why so many chose Assisi as a refuge, for it is a place with no record of any Jewish citizens.

Nearly always I received the answer that they felt drawn there by Saint Francis, and when the danger had passed many told me that they attributed their safety to him.

A boy who had been one of our most useful collaborators during the worst time wrote to his mother: "I was protected

---

[1]   This article was written by Don Aldo Brunacci in 1946. Used with permission. The book *The Assisi Underground* (American title) or *While the Pope Kept Silent* (English title) is a work of the imagination, not even loosely related to the true events.

by Our Lady and Saint Francis." They were both Jews, but she sent me the boy's letter.

With every encroachment of the German occupation more Jews arrived, and our first thought was to get them safely lodged in the various convents and with reliable families who would forget to comply with the police regulations of denouncing any strangers they had in the house.

Still, in a small place the presence of so many visitors was bound to be noted, even though Assisi then had a considerable number of non-Jewish refugees from other parts of Italy.

We felt that our Jewish friends must be protected. We provided them with false identity cards to pass them off as refugees from places already occupied by the Allies. Our chief center was the convent of San Quirico, where the visitors were generally housed until we could provide them with new ration books and all the papers which were necessary to enable them to live unmolested. Armed with these documents some of them lived with immunity in an ordinary hotel.

The printing of the documents and especially making official stamps was a difficult and risky job, but it was managed. We obtained ration books through the help of trusted friends.

When the documents and a cover-up story were ready, our refugees had to learn the geography of their new home, and were primed with every detail about local habits, personalities and gossip.

It was more difficult to provide them with the right accent and intonation and a young lady from Bari surprised hearers by answering their question in pure Venetian. Her presence of mind, however, rose to the occasion and she coolly told them of her education and upbringing in the north.

One evening a father, mother and son arrived who had escaped from a concentration camp in France. They knew no Italian and were in fact pure French. They had crossed the Alps on foot, and had been helped by the Curia in Genoa which forwarded them on to Florence whence they had been sent to Assisi for greater safety.

The secretary of the archbishop of Genoa had already provided them with documents declaring that they were Italian refugees repatriated from Tunis so we only had to find them lodging and clothes and within a week our French friends were going about quite happily and no one suspected them.

We had a difficult case in the convent when an old lady of Viennese-Jewish origin died, and it was necessary to bury her without a Catholic funeral and yet not arouse suspicion. However that, too, was managed and Frau Weiss now rests in the cemetery of Assisi under the name of Signora Bianchi.

We were particularly anxious that the Jewish boys and girls should not waste their time and, thanks to their false papers, several of them continued their studies in the public schools, while others were tutored privately and then presented themselves in the usual manner for the state examination, at which they did very well. After the liberation, of course, we corrected their names in the school records.

The idea that the Jews made a synagogue in the crypt of the very monastery founded by Saint Francis is misleading, for there is no monastery in Assisi founded by Saint Francis, and there was no synagogue in any crypt.

But it is true that in the quiet of the Assisi convents, the Jews were naturally completely free to join together for their devotions, and it often happened that while the nuns were at their prayers, close at hand, under the same roof, the Jews, too, were imploring the Divine mercy and asking God for justice and peace.

I remember how, just after the Jews had begun to arrive in Assisi on October 8, 1943, they were celebrating their Feast of Yom Kippur in the convent of San Quirico, a quiet hidden celebration of refugees. The sisters, however, had the happy inspiration of decorating the refectory and tables with flowers as for a feast and when their guests sat down to the meal after the long ritual fast and looked round, they no longer felt like strangers and understood that in the bond of charity we are all brothers and sisters.

It would take too long to tell of our many anxieties while trying to help those whom Providence sent us during those hard years. Our organization had branches in some of the small towns nearby to place refugees, for we did not want to over-populate Assisi itself. We were, of course, connected to other dioceses, for practically all the Italian clergy were working in similar ways as ourselves. Our organization was not large, but we found that it worked efficiently.

All the personal documents of our Jews, as well as their sacred books and religious objects were hidden the cellars of the palace of the Bishop of Assisi, and from beginning to end, he was the heart and soul of our work which continued until the liberation.

When I was arrested on May 15, 1944 I had a Jewish couple hidden in my house, and we were preparing the means of escape for their relations in northern Italy. I was sent to a concentration camp where other Jews were interned, but on June 4 the Allies entered Rome, and our help was no longer needed.

In all, about two hundred Jews had been entrusted to us by Divine Providence. With God's help, and through the intercession of Saint Francis, not one of them fell into the hands of their persecutors.

Valentin Müller as a student in Würzburg

COLONEL VALENTIN MÜLLER, PHYSICIAN

Josef Raischl and André Cirino

Valentin Müller was born in 1891 at Zeilitzheim in lower Franconia, Bavaria, and baptized Catholic, one of two sons of the village carpenter. In 1904, an uncle-priest encouraged him to attend the *Kilianeum*, the minor seminary at Würzburg. By 1911, having finished the *Gymnasium* level of education, he started medical school in this beautiful cathedral city. As a medical student, Müller served in World War I and was awarded the Bavarian Silver Medal for bravery in saving some injured soldiers at the front line. Unfortunately, he was imprisoned by the British army, but later liberated in a prisoner exchange. After the war he completed his studies and settled in 1919 as a medical doctor with a practice first in a little room in Emsing, Middle Franconia, and later at Titting as head doctor of a little hospital.

In 1922 he married Maria Hofer. They had two children, a son, Robert and a daughter, Irmgard, both of whom became medical doctors.

At the outbreak of World War II, Müller had already established a medical practice in Eichstätt, Oberbayern, approximately 100 kilometers (62 miles) north of Munich. He moved there in 1933 because of problems with the local

Nazi authorities in the nearby village of Titting.

In 1937, Dr. Valentin Müller purchased a house (still in the Müller family today) from a Jewish family and paid for it completely by cash, thus giving them the means to escape Germany. Moreover, Müller was the last medical doctor in Eichstätt to visit Jewish homes for treatment. He was never a member of the Nazi party.

In 1939 he was called to war again. Because of his extraordinary energy and organizational ability, he was elevated to the rank of Colonel, a rank in the health corp ordinarily restricted to professors of medicine. His son Robert described him as "a courageous, super-active man involved in everything." During this second enlistment in military service, he took part in campaigns against Poland, France and Russia.

Many years after Müller's death, letters were found in the attic of his home in Eichstätt that he wrote to his wife every other day. Excerpts from these letters give an idea of his care for all people— civilians as well as enemies—and of the stature of the man himself. From the war front he wrote:

> It is always the same experience when I enter a Russian home. I sense the fear and see the mistrust in their eyes. Then, as I softly begin to speak or touch the person gently or hold their hands to calm them down, I slowly see trust rise up in them. Their misery, pain and disease then surface, and they are simply suffering human beings, not my enemy. At this level of trust they begin to believe that they can get well if I stay with them long enough.

Unbelievably, for payment one woman wanted to give me three eggs, another woman a bit of ham, and a third one even wanted to give me money. And when I refused their gifts, they started to cry, took my hand, and kissed it out of gratitude.

In another letter he wrote: "Today I treated a four-year-old girl who was badly wounded. When I entered her home, she shouted and cried. But within a short time she became my little friend and laughed with me."

His concern for his patients had shown through in these words: "After moving to another destination, on a few occasions, I tried to return to a ten-year-old girl suffering from pneumonia and to a severely wounded woman, both of whom I had to leave behind. You can't believe how the people cried when I left. When I returned to them the first time, there were tears of joy. Thank God, both are better now."

He commented: "Because I tried to help a civilian, I got into trouble with my superiors. But I trust that every good deed will be rewarded."

Another letter recounted that he was threatened and put under surveillance by the army because of his religious beliefs: "How desperately we need the *Our Father* today, and how few pray it! For my part I need our Lord very much. Recently I corrected a soldier using foul language, and no one supported me. Nevertheless, I managed to stop him. Even though alone, I am not afraid. I respect others' opinions, but I won't tolerate an attack on what is holy to me."

In Stalingrad in 1942 he was said to have established the first military hospital. Several days before the Red Army surrounded the city, Müller was sent to Lourdes, the pilgrimage sanctuary in southern France where he had to establish a division for medical transport. As head of that division, he arrived in Italy in 1943.

While he was replacing the Medical General of the troops of southern Italy, he heard about the General's plan to establish Assisi as a hospital city. Müller succeeded in getting himself assigned to Assisi as Commander, eventually receiving more than two thousand sick and injured people.

When Müller took up his assignment in February, 1944, the closest Allied position was at Anzio, about 150 miles south of Assisi. At that time, cities of ecclesiastical and cultural significance like Assisi were not considered neutral nor exempt from war. The Benedictine Abbey of Montecassino, a cultural monument comparable to Assisi, was completely destroyed in 1944. And Assisi was deemed strategically important because of the nearby airports of Foligno and Perugia.

Very early in the war years, the Conventual friars of Assisi appealed to their General Minister in Rome, Father Bede Hess, who, with the support of the Vatican and Bishop Placido Nicolini of Assisi, approached both sides in the conflict asking them not to damage the city. On 10 July 1943, the President of the United States, Franklin D. Roosevelt, declared his country's intention not to touch the Vatican nor its possessions, which, according to the Lateran Pact, included some ecclesiastical buildings in Assisi. Later on

Arnaldo Fortini, Mayor of Assisi, contacted the Allied forces and received assurance from Field Marshall Alexander, their Commander, that Assisi would be preserved.

The German army was not willing to do the same. Müller immediately tried to cut through the red tape to obtain the status of either a hospital city or open city for Assisi, according to international law. Following the Geneva Convention of the Red Cross, no fighting forces were allowed in a hospital city. The law of the Hague stated that all military personnel must be removed from an open city. All of this must be accepted by both sides. But the German headquarters in Berlin delayed such a declaration until the front line approached the city in question, thus trying to avoid tactical disadvantages. So Müller's first efforts were in vain.

Whatever we know about his activity in Assisi, we know primarily from the citizens themselves. The *Colonnello* was esteemed and loved. He fostered good relationships with Mayor Fortini and Bishop Nicolini and he was at home with the Franciscans.

Everyone knew that whatever their need, the *Colonnello* would listen. The people knew his telephone number at the command post: 210. Müller tried with all his might to prevent any encroachment upon the city on the part of his own countrymen and when he failed to do so, he made a personal effort to repair the harm.

Once two German officers confiscated two taxis. Müller mounted his motorcycle and followed the two officers all the way to Perugia where he apprehended them and forced them to return the vehicles. Francesco Pettirossi, one of the two taxi drivers, never forgot the *Colonnello* and told everyone who it was who brought his taxi back to him.

Another time German soldiers confiscated all the bicycles they found and loaded them onto a truck. Only upon Müller's command did the soldiers unload the truck and return the bicycles. One night Müller ran to help a young woman and her children who were being harassed by drunken soldiers.

At risk to himself, he also helped the young wife of an Italian interred in a German concentration camp get a letter to her husband. He took her letter and put it in an envelope with his own name on it as the sender.

At the hospital he not only treated wounded soldiers but also cared for all the sick and injured without cost. He even made house calls!

The high esteem in which the people held him can be seen in the fact that the resistance fighters in the area around Assisi were told: "Don't touch a hair of Colonel Müller's head!"

Regarding the status of Assisi, the Medical Colonel finally took matters into his own hands. He sent the remaining troops out of the city, locked the gates at night, and placed guards as well as signs on the gates and walls prohibiting the German troops withdrawing from Italy from entering Assisi.

Müller did not have the authority to act as he did. Nevertheless, the Colonel's persistence finally paid off. On 1 June 1944, von Kessel from the German embassy advised the Vatican that Assisi was declared a hospital city. The German Ambassador to the Vatican, Ernst von Weizsäcker and the German Commander in Italy, Field Marshall Albert Kesselring, concurred.

So Assisi was left untouched when on 16 June 1944, the German Army retreated. Müller, the last one to leave, posted signs all over the city as well as leaving behind a letter to the Allied forces (the British were first to enter Assisi), pleading with them to respect the city's dignity.

Hotel Subasio, headquarters of Colonel Valentin Müller

Before withdrawing from Assisi on 17 June 1944, he arranged to have all the medical provisions—general supplies, medicine, beds, blankets and all kinds of surgical equipment worth approximately ten million lire—given to the Bishop of Assisi for him to distribute.[1] To be precise about it, on Thursday, 15 June 1944, Müller met with the Bishop and representatives of the city government in the Hotel Subasio to thank them for their hospitality. He is reported to have said: "Now at the height of reprisals, people will be tempted to regard as traitors anyone who supported the opposite side." Once again he risked life and limb by leaving the medical provisions behind.

Unfortunately, the ultimate fate of these supplies is still not clear, but it seems that when the city was liberated, the International Red Cross apparently confiscated it all, despite considerable protest from Bishop Nicolini. Don Aldo Brunacci reports that Father Rufino Nicacci, at that time the guardian of San Damiano, had a role to play in the matter:

> Rufino Nicacci is the leading character in Ramati's book, *Assisi Underground*. This is pure fiction. The author was obviously planning on a screenplay, and with this purpose in mind he could not have found a protagonist more suitable and imaginative than Fr. Rufino.

> At the end of the occupation of Assisi, Fr. Rufino and a Slovak Jew by the name of Pavel Jotza were involved in an action that was anything but judicious.

---

1   See Santucci, 103-112, *La Questione dei Medicinali.*

I am referring to the enormous supply of medical equipment that Colonel Müller so courageously and generously had given to the people of Assisi. He loved and protected our city. Father Rufino and Jotza were warned against their action by Bishop Nicolini.[2]

After being released from American imprisonment in 1945, Müller returned to Eichstätt where he continued his practice of attending daily mass at six in the morning at the Capuchin church. One day his wife did not wake him up for mass, because he had been working with an emergency through the night. So she thought he would need to sleep. But Valentin reproached her saying: "Why didn't you wake me up? You know how much I need the Eucharist."

He was esteemed as a very generous person, who helped whoever was in need. An elderly man remembered: "When I was small, my mother died and my family really had a hard time. Our father was left with nine motherless children and very little money. What I remember as if it were yesterday, unexpectedly, on Christmas Eve, Dr. Müller arrived at our home with his car full of toys. What a joyful surprise for us on that first Christmas without our Mom."

Every day Müller invited two students from poor families to his table for lunch and also gave free medical treatment to the poor.

In 1950, Müller returned with his wife, son, and daughter to Assisi. In these words from her travel journal, Irmgard,

---

2   The hand-written text of this warning appears on p. 108 of Santucci's book.

daughter of Dr. Valentin Müller, describes her father's return to Assisi: "Daddy went on alone to the Hotel Subasio. The desk clerk recognized him instantly and excitedly called the proprietors, Mr. and Mrs. Rossi. It was a wonderful welcome from a grateful people." Just six years after the departure of the German army, the former Medical Colonel and Commander of Assisi, returned to the city of Francis and Clare for a visit.

Ironically, the former occupier and enemy was practically given a hero's welcome just a few short years after the war. The former Mayor, who was in office during Müller's time, the communist Mayor, and the Bishop received him. Müller was showered with numerous invitations from the citizens of Assisi to come visit. Upon his arrival, some women placed flowers at the hotel entrance that formerly served as his headquarters. Now he and his family were invited guests of the Hotel Subasio. And the city council was planning to erect a monument in his honor.

Dr. Valentin Müller's presence was celebrated in the streets and squares of the city. People crowded around him, shaking his hand, embracing him. Why this adulation of a former German occupier? Let the people's stories and personal experience of the Colonel explain why.

In her travel journal Irmgard Müller wrote: "A woman approached us, happy and very moved, to share about the *grande paura*—the great fear—she had during the war. But when *Il Colonnello* moved into the city, the fear left her." The inhabitants of Assisi revere Müller as the city's savior. They claim it is due to his presence that the city's sanctuaries, medieval walls, treasures as well as its inhabitants, remained untouched. During the war the people used to exclaim: "We've got three protectors: God, St. Francis, and Colonel Müller."

Müller family on visit to Assisi in 1950. From left to right: Son Robert, wife Maria, Valentin, daughter Irmgard.

"My father never boasted of his heroic deeds," said his son Robert Müller, MD, who continued his father's medical practice in Eichstätt. Today Robert's son, Dominik, carries on the Müller's medical practice in Eichstätt.

Valentin Müller continued working until his death in 1951. His daughter, Dr. Irmgard Müller, remembered that while in the hospital in Munich for treatment of cancer, he received a visitor from Assisi, a friar and friend, Father Cairoli. When Cairoli entered his room and Müller saw him, he remarked: "My Assisi has come to me!" On 31 July 1951, at the age of sixty, he died of lung cancer which had traveled to his brain, and he was buried in the cemetery of Eichstätt.

Dr. Valentin Müller in Eichstätt (c. 1950)

During this time of persecution, in Italy about 32,000 Jews survived in hidden places, an estimated 300 of them in monasteries, friaries, and private homes in Assisi. Did Colonel Müller know about them? "I suppose so," said Robert Müller, MD, the Colonel's son, "and if he was deceived, then it was because he wanted to be deceived." Robert Müller was asked what would his father have done if he would have known about the Jews hidden in Assisi? His response: "Nothing. He would have allowed it because he looked at the Jews in the same way he looked at all people."

In 1984 the Jewish director, Alexander Ramati, who once came to Assisi as an Allied war journalist, made a movie about the Jews saved by the people of Assisi. The film, shot at original sites in Assisi, had Maximilian Schell portray Müller. Schell once said he would never again accept the role of a German officer in a film. Yet, learning about the integrity of Müller's person and character, he accepted the role. But Robert Müller claims his father is portrayed as "too slow and sedate, respectable, but not seeing through the situation." In Robert's opinion, his father was much more vivacious, flexible and aware than the film portrayed.

The memory of *Il Colonnello's* important role in preserving Assisi during World War II is still alive among the city's inhabitants. In 1982, a commemorative stone monument was placed in the cloister of the Würzburg Conventual friary, bearing the names of Mayor Fortini, Father Bede Hess, Bishop Nicolini and Dr. Valentin Müller. It was brought by a delegation from Assisi, led by Don Aldo Brunacci, on a pilgrimage of peace during the eighth centenary of St. Francis' birth to the first Franciscan friary established north of the Alps.

On their way the group also stopped at Eichstätt. After a reception at the City Hall, the Italians brought olive branches to Colonel Müller's grave, on whose tombstone is carved the façade of the Basilica of St. Francis. Above it are the words: *In serviendo consumor* (I give my life in serving).

In 2005 St. Bonaventure University wanted to give a posthumous service award to Colonel Valentin Müller. But before a decision to go ahead with this award was reached, the university initiated an investigation into Müller's military and political background. So the university hired a Jewish woman, Deborah E. Lipstadt, a professor at Emory University, to investigate Müller. Sr. Margaret Carney, President of St. Bonaventure University, said that at the end of Lipstadt's investigation, "she assured us that there was nothing in the background or anything negative archive-wise about Müller. In fact, all the stories seemed to be consistent. And there is no contradictory information known to us which would have been available had anyone raised an issue, which no one did."

So on 28 September 2005, an announcement came from the administration of St. Bonaventure University stating:

Sr. Margaret Carney, OSF, STD, president of St. Bonaventure University, is pleased to honor the life and service of Valentin Müller (1891-1951). Don Aldo Brunacci, a canon of the Cathedral of San Rufino in Assisi, Italy, who has been honored as a Righteous Gentile by the State of Israel, has long praised Müller's efforts to safeguard Assisi and the people within. In a preface to *The Strategy That Saved Assisi*, Don Aldo wrote: "Let us repeat that the two people most responsible for Assisi's safety were Bishop Nicolini and Colonel Müller, whose role was gratefully recognized by the city when it dedicated a street in his memory and installed a memorial plaque on Viale Vittorio Emanuele II." We share Don Aldo's praise and heed his request to remember Valentin Müller for his efforts during a most dangerous time to protect the people and the historic sanctuaries of Assisi, home to all who revere Francis and Clare, the saints who give this town its renown throughout the world.

Detail of the tombstone of Colonel Valentin Müller, depicting
the Basilica of St. Francis and the Sacro Convento

On 3 March 2014, the city of Assisi presented the
documentary film: *Uomo della Provvidenza: Il Colonnello
Valentin Müller e la Salvezza di Assisi durante la Seconda
Guerra Mondiale (A Man of Providence: Colonel Valentin
Müller and the Saving of Assisi during the Second World War).*
The film was created by Jona Raischl, great-grandson of
Colonel Müller. A woman attending, Anna Dionigi, said
when she was born in 1944, and still an infant, she was
stricken with dysentery and no medicine available locally.
Her mother took her to *Il Colonnello* who provided the cure
for her dysentery. She said: "Without the healing remedy
of Colonel Müller, I would not be standing here before
you today."

Under Dr. Valentin Müller's medical expertise, many
people experienced his healing remedies. Under Colonel

Valentin Müller's resolute leadership, Assisi was spared the massive destruction of the war machine. His consuming desire was at all costs to preserve the city of Assisi from such destruction during World War II. His desire was realized, and in doing so, he saved not only the city and its many treasures, but also the lives of its inhabitants, the many refugees, as well as an estimated 300 Jewish people.

REMEMBERING COMPASSION DURING WAR[1]

Candice Hughes

For more than 700 years pilgrims have made their way to Assisi, drawn by a tender promise of compassion. On a cold October day in 1943, Graziella Viterbi, a 17-year-old Jewish girl, found herself among them. The city of St. Francis did not disappoint her. Viterbi, her parents and her younger sister, were among the Jews saved from the ravages of the Holocaust by the Assisi underground, a network of Roman Catholic priests, nuns and lay people.

"It was the only place where they saved everyone," Viterbi says. "Not a single person was deported." The underground, now a nearly forgotten chapter of World War II, hid around 200 Jews in Assisi, secreting them in convents and monasteries and providing them with false documents, ration books, gentile names.

The Bishop of Assisi presided over the underground and his right-hand man, a young priest named Aldo Brunacci. Now 84, Brunacci looks back on those days as a golden, God-given chance to do the right thing. "Why did we do it? We did it because we had to," says Brunacci, who was later named by Israel as one of the "Righteous Among Nations,"

---

1   By Candice Hughes, Associated Press. Used with permission.

an honor bestowed on gentiles who risked their lives to save Jews from the Holocaust.

Jews started arriving in Assisi in the fall of 1943, after the German army seized control of Italy when its Axis ally dropped out of the war.

'HUNT FOR JEWS WAS ON'

"That's when the real persecution began," Viterbi recalls. "The hunt for Jews was on." The Viterbi family lived in Padua in northern Italy. They were vacationing in the mountains of northern Italy when the occupation began. "We couldn't go home. We were known there," Viterbi says.

They decided to seek refuge in an out-of-the-way place, making their way toward Assisi by car, by train and, finally, on foot. Shortly after they arrived, they ran into some people they knew from Padua, who put them in touch with Brunacci. "It was a journey guided by good fortune," Viterbi says. The priest provided them with a new identity. They became the Vitelli family from Puglia, a province in southern Italy in the hands of Allied forces. They learned how to make the sign of the cross. They invented a new family history. They boned up on Puglia's geography and customs. And they kept packed suitcases under their beds—just in case.

"Anything could be dangerous," Viterbi says. "The stupidest little thing could betray you."

On May 15, 1944, the police stormed into Brunacci's house while Viterbi's parents were there trying to arrange for safer lodging for themselves. He managed to hide the couple before the police hauled him off to a detention camp.

RELEASED TO VATICAN

The archbishop interceded on his behalf and Brunacci was released to Vatican custody on the condition he stay away from Assisi. But by June, the war was over and Brunacci was back home. The Viterbis never went back to Padua. There wasn't much to return to, even though the family had lived there for generations. More than 20 relatives had been deported to their deaths in German concentration camps. The ancient family palazzo was in ruins and there was no money to restore it. After seven years in Assisi, the family moved to Rome, where her father resumed his career as a university professor. She got a law degree, then met and married a "freethinking" Catholic. They raised two sons, the eldest now a prominent rabbi.

Then, when her husband died six years ago, Viterbi decided she'd had enough of big-city life. She moved back to Assisi, into the same apartment where her family hid during the war. She is the town's only Jewish resident. Now 72 Viterbi says she may have to move because the building needs major structural work. But she hopes to remain in the city that saved her, the city she loves.

"Assisi has always given me a sense of security."

FOOTNOTE TO ALEXANDER RAMATI'S BOOK AND FILM "ASSISI UNDERGROUND"

Aldo Brunacci

Many Italian and foreign newspapers, as well as some books which claim to have carried out historical research, (for example, a book by the Italian-American Jewish writer, Susan Zuccotti, *The Holocaust in Italy*, translated by Mondadori Publishers, 1987), in exposing the work that took place in Assisi for the salvation of the Jews, have accepted without criticism the story developed in the book and film by Alexander Ramati, *Assisi Underground*.

Since I was the only collaborator of Bishop Nicolini during the years 1943-1944 in this task, I feel it is my duty to declare that both the book and the film have completely distorted the truth.

To confirm this declaration it is enough to read an article I wrote in 1946, and a talk I gave in 1982 at the Sala della Conciliazione in Assisi on the occasion of the day dedicated to the Jewish people. Representatives of the Jewish communities of Italy, as well as authorities of Assisi were present in that hall, which was filled to capacity. It is to be noted that groups of Jews who took refuge in Assisi at that time, Alexander Ramati himself, and many citizens of

Assisi who were witnesses to the events, were among those present at this conference. Every assertion I made at that time which did not correspond to the truth could have risked receiving an uproarious denial.

Above all I am deeply distressed by the fact that Mr. Ramati's film seeks to attribute the merit for the saving of Assisi to a Slavic Jew, while that is to be attributed solely to the labors of the then Bishop of Assisi, Giuseppe Placido Nicolini, who ceded to the German Medical Command (in the person of Colonel Müller) many of the religious buildings in and around Assisi for the establishment of hospitals, obtaining in this way an authentic decree from General Kesselring. With this decree Assisi was declared a hospital city which the retreating German troops were forbidden to enter.

The work carried out for the salvation in Assisi of Jews and others under persecution had as its only center the Bishop's residence. Father Rufino Nicacci, leading character of the book and of the film, had never officially been entrusted by Bishop Nicolini with the task of saving Jews. He had never entered the Bishop's residence in that period and never had any connections either with Colonel Müller or with prelates such as, for example, the Archbishop of Florence. He was never arrested by the Germans, and the German prison in Bastia Umbra mentioned in the book never existed. Many other details were completely invented by the fantasy of the author as well as by that (none less fervid) of Fr. Rufino, who was for a long time the author's guest in Israel during the writing of the book.

Another detail, the contacts with Luigi Brizi for the

printing of the false identity cards were done under my direction and supervised by a young Jew from Trieste, Giorgio Krops. Recently, Luigi's son Trento reminded me that on a certain day in 1944, I gave him 50 Lire and my bicycle to go to Foligno to make the rubber stamps for the false identity cards. The truth about the events which took place in Assisi is much more interesting than the coarse, unlikely and romanticized story which unfortunately was taken as true, especially outside Assisi.

But this did not happen with the authoritative international magazine, *Reader's Digest*. When the book came out in the English edition, Mr. Ramati made an agreement for a good deal of money for an insertion in that magazine, presenting his book as historical.

A first examination of the book produced a very clear feeling that it was instead just a novel. In June 1978 the European Editorial Office of *Reader's Digest* telephoned from Paris to ask me if I could receive a member of its editorial staff, Dr. Denise Pilkington. After a careful inquiry into different areas of Assisi, she could not but confirm the staff's first impressions regarding the book. Before she left we read the book together for three whole days. We did not find one page that corresponded entirely to the truth. In the meantime Mr. Ramati stormed me with phone calls from Jerusalem begging me to help him not lose the large sum of money that would have been given to him by the magazine. But I couldn't lie. And so, to his great disappointment, the book was not published.

On June 23, Dr. Pilkington wrote to me from Paris saying:

"You will not be surprised to learn that we shall not publish that book!" And she added: "Because only history is worth the telling."

In various articles written and in many lectures given by me, I have always strived to restore the truth about that glorious period in the history of Assisi. But the continual spreading of these lies convinces me ever more that I must assemble and publish all the documents in my possession regarding the events in question, and this also at the request of many authoritative persons. I hope to do this as soon as possible, because only the truth deserves to be known. Moreover, on more than one occasion I have had the opportunity of bringing to the attention of important Jewish personalities I have met during these years the fact that this book does a great deal of harm to their cause, since such an enormous falsity perpetrated by a Jewish writer for the sake of gain, might make doubts arise as to the truth about what really happened during the Holocaust.

THE SECRET LETTER[1]

Delia Gallagher

Don Aldo, you are an eyewitness to a key historical event: a letter sent from the Vatican during World War II to the Catholic Bishop of Assisi, Giuseppe Nicolini (Bishop of Assisi from June 22, 1928 to November 25, 1973) in which Pope Pius XII made clear that he wanted the Bishop to help Jews about to be rounded up by the Nazis. This letter, if it existed, would be a rare, solid proof that Pius XII acted to help the Jews during the period of Nazi persecution. We would like to understand better the story of this letter, because many say that Pius XII was not interested in the destiny of the Jews, that he was "silent."

This is the greatest falsity that could be uttered! The first president of the State of Israel officially thanked Pius XII for what he did. When I was in America recently, in Buffalo, a journalist asked me about the "silence" of Pope Pius XII,

---

1   Don Aldo Brunacci with INSIDE THE VATICAN's Delia Gallagher in Assisi, May 2003. Used with permission. At 90 years old, Don Aldo Brunacci is a key witness to Pope Pius XII's intervention to assist Jews during World War II. INSIDE THE VATICAN's Robert Moynihan and Delia Gallagher went to Assisi, Italy, to question Brunacci about the day his Bishop showed him a letter from the Vatican under the signature of Bishop Giovanni Battista Montini (the future Pope Paul VI) during the reign of Pius XII.

and I responded: "Let me ask you, what is better—to act or to speak?" "To act," he responded. "Well," I said, "then let me tell you what Pius XII did for the Jews. In all the convents of Rome, in the Vatican and in the extraterritorial zones of the Vatican, there were Jews hidden in all of those places and surely all of these convents. They could not have done what they did without the Pope knowing. In the Roman seminary, where I was for seven years, there were 500 refugees, between Jews and those politically persecuted. In short, the clergy everywhere in Italy did a bit of what we did in Assisi.

But to return specifically to this letter, which you reportedly saw. When did this letter from Pius XII arrive? How did you come to see it? And how can you be certain it came from the Pope?

It was on the third Thursday of September of 1943. The Bishop called me to tell me about this letter he had received from Rome. Obviously I didn't ask him to show me the signature! He told me it was a letter from the Secretariat of State on behalf of the Holy Father.

I would like to go directly to the main point, one that has become contested: In her book, Under His Very Windows: The Vatican and the Holocaust in Italy (Yale University Press, 2001) Susan Zuccotti, who says she interviewed you, maintains that you never actually saw the text of the letter from the Vatican to Bishop Nicolini....

Ah, Zuccotti! Yes, I did speak with her. What should I say? It is true, I did not make a photocopy of the text.

Did you actually see the letter?

I did not actually see the text of the letter, but look, I was alone with the Bishop in the room, he held the letter up and showed it to me. He said he had received the letter from Rome, and he read what it said—that the Holy Father wanted us to see to it in our diocese that something would be done to ensure the safety of the Jews—and the Bishop wanted to consult with me on what to do.

So you never actually read the letter?

No, the Bishop read the letter to me.

Then, as Zuccotti suggests in her book, it might be possible that the letter was not what Bishop Nicolini told you it was, that he was in some way deceiving you?

(Brunacci laughs) Impossible, impossible. (Laughs again) It is not possible that Bishop Nicolini was deceiving me. I am certain of that. Look, we were alone in the room and he read the letter to me. It was clearly from the Vatican, there is no doubt of that. Not from the Pope himself, personally, but from the Secretariat of State. It was a letter asking the Bishop to do all he could to help the Jews, and the Bishop wanted me to advise him on the best way to carry out that request. In fact, this same order went out to many other dioceses in Italy. I have spoken with many historians, and they tell me that these letters were sent out and I think they will emerge in the coming years. I think many new documents will appear in the future, especially from the papers of Montini (the future Paul VI).

The work of Pope Pius XII was a majestic work, a work of deeds, not of words. Zuccotti doubts that Pius XII could have issued such an order because she is persuaded by the campaign launched against Pius in 1963. But that campaign has been filled with slanders and calumnies. Still, Signora Zuccotti is persuaded by it, and so cannot accept that this letter was sent out, and she has to invent the story that the Bishop deceived me to explain it away. But the letter was sent out. I saw it with my own eyes, in my Bishop's hands, as he read it to me. It was a letter from the Vatican asking the Bishop to take measures to help protect the Jews. And we took those measures.

Don't take Zuccotti too seriously. She cites the book *Assisi Underground* which is just a tissue of lies from start to finish. I know what was behind that book. But she accepts it and cites it as a reliable source.

Why did the Bishop call you to see the letter?

Well, I was called aside by the Bishop after our regular working meeting, held on the third Thursday of each month. Two steps away from the chapel where the conference had just finished was a room into which he called me secretly. He said he wanted me to carry out the request of the letter, which was to help the Jews.

What exactly did the Bishop say?

He gave me this job in the utmost secrecy. Not even the priests most close to me knew or imagined anything. Even to a person to whom I was most close, who was like a teacher to me, and saw me looking a bit distracted, I revealed nothing, because it was very dangerous.

The Bishop told me I had to help him with this work. We already had centers for Italian evacuees, so it was easy to hide Jews among four or five thousand evacuees. Those who had money, once they were given false papers, could even go to a hotel.

Anyway, during that time I saw the Bishop nearly every day. These centers for evacuees were located in the various buildings of the diocese and they were full. Sometimes even the young people of Assisi came to sleep there at night because in the morning the Germans rounded them up to make them work in the airfields at Sant'Egidio, between Assisi and Perugia.

In fact, 27 young people died in a famous bombardment of Assisi. I was the only one who went to collect their bodies with a small truck.

What was the political situation in Assisi at that time?

Well, in 1939 the Second World War began, but Italy remained out of it until 1940. I remember like it was yesterday the day we entered. I was in the study of my parish with the pastor and a professor. The piazza outside was packed with people shouting Mussolini's name, happy that he had declared war. We three were near tears, because we knew what the war would bring. Remember, Assisi was occupied not only by the Germans, but there were also Fascists who allied themselves with the Germans and became even more dangerous than before. Assisi was full of Fascist spies and we had to work in the utmost secrecy. The Fascists had a secret organization, *Opera*, to uncover traitors. They would arrest you if they heard you speaking against them.

How many Fascists were in Assisi?

I didn't count them. There weren't many but they were dangerous. You know, in a city this small, even a few bad people can do great damage! I remember one episode. I was in the cathedral and one of these Fascists came to find me because he wanted the key to one of the churches we had nearby to use for a German storehouse. I told him, I am not the boss of that church, I must ask permission of the Bishop. He began to curse the Bishop and put a gun to my throat. I turned to the German official and began to explain and the German lowered the arm of the Fascist holding the gun at my throat and said I must ask the Bishop.

What were relations like with the Jews in Assisi before the war?

Before the war, there were no Jewish families resident in Assisi. After September 8, 1943, we began to welcome them, but before that we were welcoming refugees from other parts of Italy, who were fleeing their cities that had been bombarded. At a certain point, the number of refugees equaled the number of residents.

How many Jews were refugees in Assisi?

Unfortunately, I didn't keep any records at that time. It was too dangerous. But if I calculate that in Assisi we had one center, then another in Perugia with a parish, I would say a total of 250-300 Jews.

Of these 250-300, how many were taken by the Nazis?

None. Last summer I went to New Jersey for a conference with 350 people in a synagogue and I concluded my talk citing a Paduan professor, of Jewish origin, who said: "We will tell our children the story of Assisi, because all those who passed through were saved; no one was lost." The New Jersey newspaper that reprinted my talk entitled it, "No one was lost."

Where were they housed?

All over. Mainly in the guest houses of the convents. I remember taking the first family to a convent of German nuns. I am still in contact with the daughter of this family who lives in Israel. She sent me a book she wrote about the time there.

They were also housed privately with families. They needed

identification papers in order to go out and especially to get food. Bread, sugar, everything was rationed. So we had to provide them with false papers, citing free cities in the south of Italy as the place of birth.

The Germans didn't catch on to the false documents?

They were very well done! They were made by a typographer in Assisi who had a manual machine. We gave each one a family name from the south of Italy.

You personally were involved in distributing false documents?

Of course!

How?

I remember once I gave my bicycle and 50 lire to the typographer and his son to go to Foligno to my friend who would stamp and wrap them. A young Jewish boy was in charge of keeping all the papers in order at my house so they would be ready for me to distribute.

What happened to the original Jewish documents?

The real documents of the Jews, along with their valuables and jewelry, were put in the cellar of the Bishop's house. The door was covered over with a wall that the Bishop himself had built with his own hands. The Bishop was a holy man and followed the precept *ora et labora*, and he knew how to do manual work. While he constructed the wall, I held the candle because there was no electricity in the cellar.

What happened when the cellar was opened?

All the documents and valuables were given back.

When did that happen?

After the war. A few times, during the war, I had to re-open the wall because some families moved. I opened and closed it immediately, always at night. I used to go from Perugia to Assisi by bicycle carrying documents to families that had moved. We made appointments at the church of Santa Susanna in Perugia. I went there at night and slept in the attic with some of the young Jews in hiding and left early in the morning to be back for school at 8:30 a.m. To make it up the hills, I sometimes grabbed on to German army trucks and let them carry me up! Back then, priests often travelled by bicycle, so I didn't raise any suspicions.

Is it possible to visit the cellar of the Bishop's house?

Well, the house was completely redone after the earthquake. For four years, the Bishop didn't live there. The cellar area still exists, but it has been made into offices and cleaned up.

Just before the war ended you were arrested.

Yes, Assisi was liberated June 17, 1944, but I wasn't there. I had been arrested May 15, 1944, and was put in a type of concentration camp. Thanks to the intervention of the archbishop of Perugia, and the fact that they were moving the camp, I was able to escape 10 days later.

Why were you arrested? Did they discover something?

Nothing in particular; they were very suspicious but didn't have any evidence. They threatened to take me north but didn't have time.

Then you were summoned to work in Rome?

I went to Rome at the end of May. (Bishop Giovanni Battista) Montini had asked me to work at the Vatican in the Relief Office. The Relief Office took care of political prisoners so in a certain sense I continued the work I was doing in Assisi.

I remember the time after celebrating Mass for some young people at the end of May, the police arrested me as I was coming out of the church. They accompanied me back to my house before taking me to the camp, and I remembered that in my study I had a Jewish university professor and his wife who were looking for another place to stay because they did not feel safe where they were. Fortunately, the police waited for me at the bottom of the stairs and did not come up to my study. I took my things and closed the door behind me.

I am still in contact with the daughters of this couple: one lives in Israel and is married to a diplomat—she called me just a few nights ago. The other is in Rome, and one of her sons is a famous rabbi who lectured, together with Cardinal Martini, at the University of Milan.

Do you remember the liberation of Rome?

Yes, June 4th, 1944, was the liberation of Rome and from the Relief Offices which were near the front of St. Peter's I could see General (Mark) Clark coming up the stairs of St. Peter's in his jeep.

I saw St. Peter's Square and the Via della Conciliazione fill up with crowds who had come to thank Pius XII. There were many Jews among them! The question of Pius XII arose after 1963, and no one knows why. For what reason did they need a scapegoat?

DON ALDO WAS RIGHT! [1]

André Cirino

Just barely coming to grips with Don Aldo's death , I was reading *The Times* here in England and I could almost feel Don Aldo tapping me on the shoulder to read the article on page 27 entitled: "The KGB and the Plot to Taint the 'Nazi Pope'" (18/02/07), which opened:

> The KGB hatched a plot to smear the late Pope Pius XII as an anti-semitic Hitler supporter and fostered a controversial play that tarnished the pontiff, according to the highest-ranking Soviet bloc intelligence officer to have defected to the West, former Lieutenant-General Ion Mihai Pacepa...who broke a silence of nearly half a century to reveal he was involved in the operation...a Kremlin scheme launched in 1960 to portray Pius XII "as a cold-hearted Nazi sympathizer."

Whenever I invited Don Aldo to address our pilgrims about Assisi and its involvement concealing many Jewish people during World War II, he would inevitably begin by recounting an incident that occurred at a clergy meeting in

---

1   Written by André Cirino, OFM shortly after the death of Don Aldo Brunacci 2 February 2007.

Assisi during the war.

Bishop Niccolini called him out of the meeting to show him a letter that he received from the Vatican from Bishop Montini (the future Paul VI) urging Bishop Niccolini to offer lodging to all refugees, especially Jewish refugees. Because of that letter from the Vatican, Don Aldo always maintained that Pius XII had helped the Jewish people find refuge in many a Catholic institution, especially then and there in Assisi.

Don Aldo always said that it was not safe to keep the letter the Bishop read to him, and he never saw it again.

Moreover, Don Aldo claimed that Pius XII worked quietly behind the scenes, especially after the fierce reaction of the Nazi government to an open letter from the Dutch bishops which resulted in the seizure of thousands, mostly Jews, to be sent off to concentration camps. Don Aldo believed that Pius XII chose to avoid a larger arrest and imprisonment by acting quietly, behind the scenes.

And the *The Times* proved him right!

UNIVERSITY HONORS ITALIAN PRIEST FOR HELPING JEWS IN WORLD WAR II[1]

Father Aldo Brunacci, a canon of the Cathedral of San Rufino in Assisi, Italy, received St. Bonaventure University's national Gaudete Medal March 25 in Washington for helping Jews escape the Nazis during World War II.

"Don Aldo's bravery in the face of grave personal danger represents service to others at the highest level, that of selfless giving," said Franciscan Father Dominic Monti, interim president of St. Bonaventure University in New York state. Father Monti and the university's president-elect, Franciscan Sister Margaret Carney, attended an exhibit at the U.S. Holocaust Memorial Museum with Father Brunacci before presenting him with the award.

During World War II Father Brunacci helped house, feed, hide, and educate 200 Jews in homes and monasteries in Assisi. With the help of others, he arranged for these family members to obtain false documents that would help them escape. The priest also hid Jewish families in his own residence. On May 15, 1944, the Fascists arrested Father Brunacci and transported him to a concentration camp,

---

1   CATHOLIC ONLINE – U.S. NATIONAL NEWS, March 30, 2004. Used with permission. See also THE EAST TENNESSEE CATHOLIC, April 11, 2004: www.etcatholic.com/apr11/jews.

but they never discovered the family hiding in his home. Soldiers freed the priest and other prisoners one month later.

Israel awarded Father Brunacci the medal of the Righteous Gentile for his efforts. He has been recognized by the Yad Vashem Museum and Research Center in Israel and the Holocaust Museum in Washington. The Assisi diocesan priest is also part of an archival film project directed by Steven Spielberg that focuses on Holocaust victims and those who helped them.

Father Brunacci currently operates the Pope John XXIII house, a major retreat house in Assisi, and a bookstore featuring Franciscan and medieval scholarship. He is also a respected Greek and Latin classicist and author.

GAUDETE MEDAL AWARD
ST. BONAVENTURE UNIVERSITY
MARCH 25, 2004[1]

Severin Hochberg

For the Jews in Italy, the Holocaust began in the fall of 1943, when the Germans took over the central and northern regions of the country. They established a puppet Italian government, the Republic of Salò, and began measures against the 37,000 Italian and 8,000 foreign Jews in their territory. Arrests and deportations of Jews were carried out with more than 7,000 being arrested and held in local jails and concentration camps, and deported to Auschwitz.

Without help from ordinary Italians, the Jews would not have survived, and no group was more helpful than the monks, priests, and nuns of the Roman Catholic Church. They hid the Jews and partisans in convents and monasteries, and in remote villages. They established underground networks to move people quickly from place to place, and provided money, false documents, and ration cards. Priests suspected of hiding Jews and partisans were treated with special brutality by Germans and Fascists. 170 priests were murdered in reprisals. In the words of historian Susan

---

1   Editors' note: Excerpts from the speech by Severin Hochberg, historian of the U.S. Holocaust Memorial Museum: see www.sbunews.sbu.edu/Gaudete. Used with permission.

Zuccotti, the Italian clergy demonstrated great courage and compassion.... "Theirs was an altruism that lay people may often expect from the religious, but that can never he taken for granted. In Italy, most men and women of the Church were a credit to their calling."

In Assisi, a town of 5000, at least 200 Jews, none of whom had any previous connection to the town, were rescued by an effort carried out by its clergy. While the initiative was that of Bishop Giuseppe Nicolini, it was Don Aldo Brunacci, Canon of the Cathedral of San Rufino, who coordinated the effort. Father Brunacci was assisted by Fathers Rufino Nicacci and Michele Todde, Mother Giuseppina of the Poor Clare Convent at San Quirico, and others in a network that gave shelter to Jews until June 17, 1944 when the Allies liberated Assisi. Don Aldo ran a clandestine school for the Jewish children. He was arrested on May 15, 1944 and taken to a concentration camp. At the time of his arrest, he was hiding a Jewish couple in his own house. Not a single Jew was betrayed in Assisi and no attempt was made to convert them. Jews were able to gather to pray and to celebrate their religious holidays quietly in the convent of San Quirico.

Don Aldo wrote, speaking of the region around Assisi: "We were of course, in connection with other dioceses, for practically all the Italian clergy were working on similar lines as ourselves." Jews were able to survive during the Holocaust, with the assistance of local people, and of clerics such as Don Aldo Brunacci and his colleagues, who at great risk, put into practice their love and concern for their fellow human beings.

ASSISI PRIEST HONORED IN WASHINGTON FOR PROTECTING JEWS DURING WORLD WAR II[1]

Gerard Perseghin

Ninety years old, alert and possessing a great sense of humor, Don Aldo Brunacci of Assisi, Italy, remembers the German occupation of Assisi, a world-renowned repository of faith and art, the way it actually was in 1943-44 and not the way it has been depicted in films.

The priest hid Jews in cloistered convents; he invited them to attend Christmas Midnight Mass in order to quell suspicion about their identity; he even taught them in the schools and when one died a natural death, he saw her buried under a fictitious identity which was later changed.

He was the Canon of Bishop Giuseppe Placido Nicolini at the Cathedral of San Rufino in Assisi and the Bishop's right-hand man. Together they saved hundreds of Jews as well as other refugees who poured into Assisi during World War II, looking for asylum. They had some help from Colonel Valentin Müller, a German physician, head of German forces in Assisi for nearly a year, and reportedly a devout Catholic who was forced to serve the Nazi forces;

1   By Gerard Perseghin in: THE CATHOLIC UNIVERSITY OF AMERICA (www.catholicstandard.org). Used with permission.

without Nazi sympathies, he apparently turned a blind eye to the comings and goings of Jews trying to escape under the guidance of Don Aldo and the Bishop.

Recently Don Aldo, the only surviving lead character in this drama, was honored here in Washington. He gave the opening prayer in the U.S. House of Representatives on March 24 and then on March 25, 2004, he was honored by the Holocaust Memorial Museum in Washington. He presented Sara Bloomfield, the museum's director, with a decorative tile with a Latin inscription.[2] He then toured the museum and visited with Holocaust survivors.

For housing, hiding, feeding and schooling hundreds of Jews in monasteries and convents in Assisi, the priest has been honored by the State of Israel, which gave him the Medal of the Righteous Gentile, and by the Yad Vashem Museum and Research Center there. He is also part of Steven Spielberg's archival film project focusing on Holocaust survivors and the "righteous gentiles" who helped them.

St. Bonaventure University in upstate New York recently honored the priest scholar with their National Gaudete Medal for his "service to God and humanity in the Franciscan spirit of compassion and sacrifice, joy and hope." The Franciscan-sponsored University brought him to Washington, where he talked about his experiences sixty years ago.

Though not a Franciscan himself—he is a diocesan priest— Don Aldo sat in his room at the Grand Hyatt downtown

---

2   Editors' note: *Pax et bonum! Peace and all good!* A greeting of St. Francis of Assisi that has become a summation of his theology and spirituality.

and talked about how he is a "Franciscan at heart." Speaking a little English, he resorted to Italian most of the time and was assisted by an interpreter.

Don Aldo pointed out that when the government fell in Assisi, the Bishop had to step in, explaining why the Bishop and his top Canon or aide had to take the lead in helping the Jews. Assisi is a small hilltop town that was fortunately not bombed during the war. As a result, refugees poured into this village-like setting where "people were sympathetic," said Don Aldo.

On September 8, 1943, when the Nazi occupation of Assisi began, Bishop Nicolini received, as Don Aldo said, "an official letter from the Vatican Secretary of State under Pope Pius XII asking the people of Assisi to do everything they could to help all refugees, in particular the Jews." At that point the Bishop called Don Aldo and showed him the letter and asked him to take charge of caring for the Jews. Don Aldo pointed out that Assisi has many religious communities there with houses of hospitality for pilgrims. "For the Jews the problem was not resources, but hiding their Jewish identity," he said. First the Bishop and priest got them counterfeit identity cards, so they could get ration cards. He recalled how one French family arriving in Italy got new Italian identity cards that showed they were of Italian extraction coming from the French colony of Tunisia in North Africa.

"The problem was the Jews came with books, Bibles, and so on which could identify them. Rabbis had liturgical garb," said Don Aldo. The Bishop's residence was large, so Bishop

Nicolini, who was an accomplished stone mason, put all the Jewish materials in part of the basement and then with Don Aldo holding a candle, he sealed it up in a room. When the Bishop tired from his masonry work, Don Aldo took up the trowel and cement and worked while the Bishop held the candle.

Because so many of the Jews were put up in houses of hospitality, they had to be moved occasionally to make it look as if they were pilgrims. Italian guest houses also had to declare visitors within 24 hours of their arrival and registration.

At other times the Bishop allowed the Poor Clare community of religious women to hide Jews in their cloister which in those days was behind grates. "The Jews would dress in the habits of the Poor Clares" when they went for a walk outside, said Don Aldo. Even a baby was born in Assisi during the year of the occupation.

When a Jewish family needed their money which was stored away in the sealed basement room, Don Aldo got it, and rode his bike to nearby Perugia where the family was hiding. On the way back he got a ride holding onto a German military vehicle. "So the Nazis didn't know they were helping," laughed Don Aldo.

The priest, who was also a teacher of classic languages such as Latin, Greek and Hebrew, also taught the Jewish children. In his hotel room here, he told an enthralled audience how one of those young women, now in her 70s, visited Don Aldo in Assisi last year and brought her journal which recorded those days.

Don Aldo said no one ever applied pressure to convert the Jews to Catholicism. "The only (intention)," he said, "was to save them."

When he asked some Jews why they came to Assisi, they said that they "trusted in St. Francis," who was the most famous resident of that fanciful, art-endowed, and faith-filled town.

DON ALDO BRUNACCI DISCUSSES HIS EFFORTS TO SAVE 200 JEWS DURING WORLD WAR II[1]

Bob Edwards

Don Aldo Brunacci of Assisi is an Italian Catholic priest who helped save more than 200 Jews during World War II. His work began in 1943 in Assisi just after German bombers had destroyed much of the surrounding countryside. While assisting thousands of Italian refugees who flooded the city, Don Aldo and other local priests also sheltered and fed Jews. Don Aldo is 90 years old. I spoke with him last week after he received a medal from St. Bonaventure University at the Holocaust Memorial Museum here in Washington. Through an interpreter, Don Aldo said the Nazi's brutal Italian campaign actually helped him save Jews.

Given those thousands of refugees in Assisi, it was much easier to hide a few hundred other people, in this case, Jewish. The Bishop and I created a committee to organize the sheltering of all those people.

---

1   By Bob Edwards, NATIONAL PUBLIC RADIO, Morning Edition on March 31, 2004. Used with permission. Don Aldo Brunacci spoke in Italian and was translated by Jean François Godet-Calogeras.

There were so many homeless, hungry Italian Catholics. Why risk your life for a couple of hundred Jews?

Well, the answer to that question is simple. It is what the Gospel asks a Christian to do.

Those Jews who were sheltered by the Catholic clergy in Italy were able to practice their faith. Was that ever a question?

No, there was absolutely no question to prevent them from practicing their religion. They went through interesting stories like an elderly Jewish woman who died and they had to bury her. But they didn't do anything to look like they were practicing Christian religion. As a matter of fact, it was in the wintertime, so they were helped by that. They arrived at the cemetery and it was very cold, and so everything had to go very fast. Don Aldo said to the people at the cemetery: "Well, we already did everything before, so we just put the body in and that's it."

I heard a story that the Bishop knew masonry work and that the two of you were building false walls so you could hide documents behind them.

The problem was that with Jewish families, not only did you have to give them a new identity and an identity card but you had to hide their Jewish belongings. The residence of the Bishop is a big house, so they went in the basement, they had different cellars, and they put everything in there. Don Aldo was holding the candle because there was no electricity down there and the Bishop was laying bricks with cement. And then when the Bishop was tired, the Bishop would hold the candle and Don Aldo would continue.

There was a funny story that was circulating in Assisi at some point that the Bishop and Don Aldo had buried two Jewish people in that place.

We've heard so often over the years of charges that the Church was not only insensitive to the plight of the Jews but perhaps even complicit in what happened to them. What we heard today from the museum historian was that the Church was very active in saving Jews. Why is this story still contradicted by so many authors today?

In September 1943, the Bishop of Assisi received a very classified letter from the Secretary of State of the Vatican asking the Bishop to organize help to take care of all the refugees, especially the Jews. Don Aldo says that Pope Pius XII, who was pope at that time, did unbelievable things to save Jews. And as a matter of fact, there recently was published a list of church organizations, religious communities, who saved Jews during those years. Just in Rome alone there were thousands.

Well, you were arrested by the Fascists. Were you— how were you caught? Were you betrayed?

No, he was not betrayed, but he was suspected. And the suspicion became so high that one day he was coming back home and he saw the police. At that point, he had a Jewish family in his house, and it was really fortunate that the police just waited outside. So they arrested him outside and took him without realizing that there were Jews in the house.

Did you think after you were arrested that you would survive until the Allied liberation?

He was arrested May 15. Three weeks later, not even, on June 4, Rome was liberated by the Allied troops. He was not kept in Assisi. They wanted to move him north, which of course would have been worse, but they took him to Rome. And that was his salvation because then Rome was liberated.

We've spoken here today about 200 Jews, and of course with children, grandchildren perhaps even great-grandchildren, that number is much, much greater. Do you think about that? Do you think about the numbers?

Yes, he thinks of that, and there is no way he couldn't because he remained in contact with those who are still alive or their children and grandchildren. Not long ago there came a Jewish woman who is now 70. She was 14 when she was rescued by Don Aldo with her family. And she came and brought to Don Aldo the journal that she was writing in those years.

ASSISI, 1943[1]

Edward Kislinger

It's the start of a new day in Assisi. A chorus of church bells echoes off the well-scrubbed streets. Flowers overflow from the window boxes, cascading down pink stone walls. The Piazza del Comune, the town's small historic center, is already beginning to fill with the day's visitors.

If Disneyland is the happiest place on earth, then Assisi is a close second. And it owes it all to its favorite son, St. Francis, Italy's larger-than-life patron saint. His "enchanting nature," as Pope John XXIII put it, "seems to hover in the air," attracting thousands of pilgrims and tourists every year. But during the Nazi occupation, which ended sixty years ago in June, Assisi attracted thousands of desperate refugees. For some it was life-saving.

I'm sitting at an outdoor café in the piazza with one of those refugees, Graziella Viterbi, a Jewish grandmother with a mane of short white hair and bright, engaging eyes. She orders Coca-Colas for both of us and with a thoughtful smile tells me: "Assisi's been my home for fifty-six years."

"My family name is from the town of Viterbo near Rome,"

---

1   By Edward Kislinger in: COMMONWEAL, October 8, 2004. © 2004 Commonweal Foundation reprinted with permission.

she says. "We have been in Rome before Christ or perhaps when Titus destroyed the Temple." As she speaks, I can't help but imagine her as a girl in the innocent days before the war.

Graziella arrived in Assisi in October 1943, shortly after Italy's sudden surrender to the Americans and the Brits. Already angered by the Italian government's refusal to hand over Jews, Hitler had turned on his former ally with a vengeance. The Nazis occupied the country and the Viterbis fled Padua, the family's home for five hundred years, where her father, Emilio Viterbi, was a professor of chemistry and dean of the University of Padua, which was founded while St. Francis was still alive.

Emilio was an admirer of Francis and kept a copy of inspirational stories from the saint's life by his bed. Perhaps, he thought, if they could reach Assisi, two hundred miles to the south, they could find shelter. When they arrived, they found the SS, the Gestapo, and the Italian Fascist police relaxing at the Café Excelsior, the wartime name of the café where Graziella and I are seated. Unsure of where to turn, Emilio sought help from Bishop Nicolini of Assisi. He was "a loving man," she tells me, "like a boy in his enthusiasm, clever with a wonderful heart." He told her father: "There is no room left except my bedroom and my office. However, I can make do and sleep in the office. The bedroom is yours."

Graziella pauses as an elderly but sprightly nun hurries past our table carrying a bag of fruits and vegetables. She nods mischievously in her direction and tells me that Nicolini had already filled Assisi's convents and churches with hundreds of Jews disguised as monks and nuns. I laugh at the thought of matzo ball soup warming on the convent kitchen stove. She shrugs and replies that at the convent of San Quirico, "the nuns even prepared a dinner celebrating the ending of the fast on Yom Kippur," the holiest day on the Jewish calendar.

Others hid in plain sight. Don Aldo Brunacci, Nicolini's assistant, provided the Viterbis with new identity papers (the Bishop kept the originals behind a picture of the Madonna on the wall behind his desk) and found them a room in a local hotel. He also enrolled seventeen-year-old Graziella and her sister in the Catholic school he headed, where their teacher taught them prayers so that they could attend Mass and take the traditional evening *passeggiata* stroll between the churches of St. Francis and St. Clare.

The café check arrives Italian style, folded in half under a cup. We walk toward the Hotel Belvedere on Via Borgo Aretino, passing upscale boutiques along the way. I smell fresh-baked bread, olive oil, garlic, and basil. We talk about the years after the war. Graziella married a Catholic and their son became a rabbi.

She stops at a shop on Via Santa Chiara, one of the many stores selling postcards and ceramics. A hundred-year-old printing press sits in the front window. This, she tells me, was used to print the false identity papers that were provided by Brunacci for her and the hundreds of other Jews living in the city.

Graziella points out an apartment building down the block. Her family moved there fifty-six years ago after the police began making inquiries at the hotel where they were then staying. After the war, the Viterbis remained in Assisi, becoming the first Jewish family to live there.

Graziella thanks me for coming to talk to her but adds, sadly: "Even in Italy, few people know what happened." I want to say that they will, but only time will tell.

"HIDDEN IN ASSISI AND SAVED BY A PRIEST."[1]

Maurizio Baglioni

"Fate urged us on towards Assisi and that was fortunate for us. My family was saved, along with a few hundred other Jews who sought refuge there, finding hospitality from religious and civilians who risked their lives for us." This is how Graziella Viterbi, recalls her experience in the city of St. Francis in September, 1943. She was seventeen years old. She had come from Padua with her Jewish family— her father, Emilio, a university professor, her mother, Margherita, and her younger sister, Miriam. They sought refuge after 8 September.

Today Assisi is known as "The World Capital of Peace" and is the bearer of strong values. It is often the scene of major events with immense visual and media impact. At that time, however, with the saving of many Jews in the convents and homes of the Seraphic city, it saw the silent effort of concrete brotherhood, love of neighbor, and the ability to help those in need, even at the risk of one's own life. These stories make tangible the values that the land of St. Francis symbolizes today. This work involved the clergy and religious—Bishop Giuseppe Placido Nicolini,

---

1   Interview with Graziella Viterbi, by Maurizio Baglioni, IL RESTO DEL CARLINO, 27 January 2009. Translated by Nancy Celaschi, OSF. Used with permission.

Don Aldo Brunacci, Padre Rufino Niccacci, Padre Michele Todde, the sisters of the various convents, and the German Colonel, Valentin Müller, who spared no effort to have Assisi declared a hospital city.

"Under totally casual circumstances my parents had learned that Assisi was a quiet place and decided to go there," Viterbi said. "We took rooms in a hotel and there we met someone we knew from Padua. We learned that there was an underground movement led by Bishop Nicolini helping the Jews. We made contact with the movement and we became friends with Bishop Nicolini and also with Don Aldo Brunacci and Padre Niccacci. We succeeded in obtaining false identity papers printed by the Brizis, and we managed to obtain lodging with a family in the area of the city called *Borgo Aretino*. We were saved, along with about another hundred Jews who had been given refuge in the convents and monasteries. I remained living in that same house until about ten years ago."

Assisi became a safe refuge because of the activities of the members of that movement and some favorable coincidences. "Our suitcases were always packed, ready to leave for the concentration camp," Viterbi explained. "They came looking for us at the hotel where we had registered under our real names, but the owner told them that we had already gone away. I also recall when Don Aldo Brunacci was arrested; we were with him, but he managed to hide us in his study."

When asked about the roles of Bartali[2] and Colonel Müller,

---

2   Gino Bartali was a champion road cyclist. He was the most renowned Italian

she replied: "I can't say with any certainty if Gino Bartali had a role in the affair, carrying documents between Assisi and Florence. As for Müller, I personally think that he knew what was going on. This is why we always maintained contact with him and his family, and when we visited Eichstätt, we placed an olive branch on his grave."

cyclist before the Second World War, having won the Giro d'Italia three times and the Tour de France in 1938.

THE JEWS SAVED IN THE SHADOW OF THE POVERELLO[1]

Mario Roncalli

It may seem like a tired old plot, but this time it's absolutely true. However, in reading the pages written by Mirjam Viterbi Ben Horin, entitled *Con gli occhi di allora (Seen with the Eyes of the Past)*, at times it seems that you are not reading a true story but more so a novel. However, this is not the case. The author is narrating a horror story, but one with moments of joy and a happy ending which, unfortunately, is not often the case. The story is hers, but one shared by many other Jews who, during the Nazi occupation, found unwavering help in the homeland of St. Francis. It is, surprisingly, light reading with a careful style, but heavy because of the many episodes that lose nothing because of their gravity. Each page contains distant memories and unforgettable emotions, clear word images accompanied, as it were, by captions describing the emotions.

Two parts of this small but precious book are inspired by a liberating need to tell the truth and express gratitude. The first part speaks about a childhood in Padua (1938-1943) and a little girl forced to become gradually more aware of the growing discrimination to which her family was subjected

---

1   This book review of *Con gli occhi di allora* by Mirjam Viterbi Ben Horin was written by Mario Roncalli, for L'Avvenire, 4 October 2008. Translated by Nancy Celaschi, OSF. Used with Permission.

after the passage of racist laws (her father's expulsion from the university, her sister's departure from high school, the gradual disappearance of friends and acquaintances). It speaks about a child in exile obliged to study the piano, lessons that were seen as both a means of survival and soon a source of unhappiness.

The second part concerns her stay in "the city of the saint" following September 8. She remembers the visible disturbances of a star of David, a life-size-hanged-man in red paint on the entrance of their house, as well as the fire at the great synagogue which stopped short of the Aron ha Kodesh sparing the scrolls of the Torah. Now, in the "city of the Poverello," in 1943-44, we can follow the moves of the Viterbi family from the Hotel Sole where, for the first and only time, they could register with their own identity papers with the notation "Jewish family," to their other provisional accommodations where they lived clandestinely after the racist laws were intensified.

And here again we can almost relive the fears of the parents and their two daughters, the impact of Assisi on Mirjam and her family with its stones, olives, ceramic art, and more importantly its inhabitants. She notes those Catholic "brethren" united in a clandestine organization led by Bishop Giuseppe Placido Nicolini with Don Aldo Brunacci, Padre Rufino Nicacci, the printers Luigi and Trento Brizi (all later recognized among "the Just Ones") and with other priests from nearby places such as Don Federico Vincenti in Perugia, who, at the height of the anti-Semite furor, did not hesitate, with Mayor Arnoldo Fortini as an accomplice, to help the Viterbis and other Jewish families by providing them with those most precious false identity documents. Later on they provided them with a series of imaginary names when the search of the printing shops revealed some irregularities. Mirjam Viterbi became Mirella Varelli, then Maria Vitelli, etc. They were offered safe hiding places, starting with the bishop's house, a shelter for an incredible number of evacuees and persecuted persons in addition to serving as a secret storage area for Jewish objects. These safe havens included San Damiano where some Jews dressed in friars' habits, San Quirico, San Rufino, and other dwellings procured for them by the secret Catholic network.

"I began to understand that there was something connecting me, a hidden little Jewish girl, and the patron saint of Italy. There was a blessing" writes Mirjam Viterbi, who still recalls the warmth of those presences in her life at that time, when it did not seem strange at all for her to "go to Mass every Sunday" in the beautiful churches of Assisi "in order not to arouse suspicion" and make the sign of the cross, or rather, "some movement similar to a cross, but which really wasn't one. And it wasn't one bit blasphemous, neither for the Catholic religion, nor for ours." Then she added: "I was in absolute peace with myself. And that's how it was when I would enter the church and go through the motions of dipping my fingers into the holy water, without touching it. They told me that in certain cases God watches the movement of the hearts, not the hands. And my heart was filled with respect in both directions. I was forced to do certain things, and I had to understand this."

Her story continues, recounting the arrest of her friend, Don Aldo Brunacci by the Fascist police, and then the advance of the allied forces up to the point of the liberators' entry into the city: "They entered to the applause of all, with no martial airs, one by one. I heard someone behind me grumbling, 'This one is cannon fodder.' I did not immediately understand those words. But then there was a new difficult reality, a painful awareness that struck me inside like a fist. I could have cried, but fortunately my eyes remained dry, and I continued to smile, to celebrate, like everyone else." What happened after that day is described by that once little Jewish girl who later became a noted neuropsychiatrist and active participant in Jewish-Christian dialogue, belongs to "another phase of her life" or perhaps we should say, to "another life" that cannot be described with "the eyes of the past."

THE COURAGE OF A RIGHTEOUS ONE IN THE CITY OF SAINT FRANCIS[1]

Gaetano Vallini

It was a Thursday at the end of September 1943. The Bishop called me aside. "I received instructions from the Vatican Secretariat of State," he said to me; "they asked me to offer aid and assistance to those being persecuted, particularly the Jews. This is Pope Pius XII's desire." He urged me to the greatest caution. No one must know anything. From that day onward Assisi's convents and religious communities began to hide hundreds of Jews.

Thus, in his last newspaper interview, one given several days before his death last Friday[2] at the age of 92, Don Aldo Brunacci recalled the beginning of that great operation of solidarity that saved the lives of some 300 Jews. For that courageous humanitarian work, in 1977, Israel conferred on Don Aldo Brunacci, together with Bishop Giuseppe Nicolini, the title of "Righteous among the Nations," while in 2003 the President of the Republic of Italy designated him a "Knight of the Grand Cross."

---

1   This article from the official Vatican newspaper was written after the "Interview with Don Aldo Brunacci" by Paolo Mirti included in this book. While Vallini repeats some of Mirti's interview, he includes other details the editors wanted to preserve. Gaetano Vallini, L'OSSERVATORE ROMANO, February 5-6, 2007. Translated by Nancy Celaschi, OSF. Used with permission.

2   February 2, 2007.

As is recounted in the recent book by Paolo Mirti, *La societá delle mandorle*[3], it all began on September 8, 1943, when a steady stream of refugees began arriving in Assisi, eventually reaching the number of 6,000. In response to the emergency the Bishops' office set up a Refugee Assistance Committee.

When Bishop Nicolini called upon him, Don Aldo was a 29-year-old Canon of the Cathedral of San Rufino. He was the son of a rope-maker and housewife who also supplemented the family income as a seamstress. The Brunacci family made many sacrifices to allow their son to study and to help develop the vocation that gradually became evident. He did his best to repay his parents, earning his degree in theology at a pontifical major seminary in Rome.

"Don Aldo," Mirti notes, "was certainly not a person dear to the Fascist regime. His rather limited inclination to flattery, combined with a profound learning that some people mistook for intellectual pride, definitely made him a troublesome priest." It is no surprise then, as was later revealed, that the noon Mass he celebrated was regularly attended by agents of the Fascist secret police who listened to his sermons to discover any subversive parts. Among other things, Father Brunacci also espoused the ideas of Catholic Action and, in accord with his undeniably not very diplomatic character, never missed the opportunity to show it.

Therefore, it was no accident that Don Aldo was the first person to whom the Bishop would reveal his plan to help

---

3   *The Almond Society*, Giustina, 2007.

the Jews, and he saw him as the person who could best help him organize it. The young priest did not hesitate to agree and threw himself into the project without delay. Thus, along with the Committee for the Refugees, he began to set up a secret parallel organization whose purpose was to offer protection to the Jewish refugees mixed in among the thousands of evacuees.

Everything went ahead under the direction of Bishop Nicolini, a 65-year-old native of Trentino who, as Don Aldo Brunacci never failed to emphasize, was the person really behind the massive work of saving the Jews. Before becoming a bishop, he was a Benedictine monk, and he assumed the responsibility of opening the doors of the convents and monasteries and, in case of necessity, even their enclosures, to the Jews. The headquarters of the organization was the Poor Clare Monastery of San Quirico. The persecuted were housed there and in the guest houses of the Colettines, the Stigmatines, the German Capuchin sisters and the Benedictines of Sant'Apollinare until the committee managed to procure new identity cards for them, giving them the right to receive ration cards. With these false documents some of them were able to live undisturbed in hotels or private apartments.

It was often necessity to hide "dangerous" objects: sacred books, family mementos, liturgical objects. Don Aldo and Bishop Nicolini hid them in the basement of the bishop's house, in recesses that they then walled up. "Bishop Nicolini personally did the bricklaying while I held the candle. When it was time to break into the wall, I assumed that work," Don Aldo recalled.

From the start the biggest problem was that of the documents; they had to obtain false ones. The Bishop collaborated with Padre Rufino Niccacci, who had shortly before been named Guardian of the friary of San Damiano. He asked this friar, who in 1974 was also named one of the "Righteous of the Nations," to approach an openly communist printer, Luigi Brizi, who was willing, and, despite the risk, also involved his son Trento.

Obviously, everything was conducted in great secret and it was impossible to be too careful. Everyone and everything was suspect. Then, too, it was necessary always to be ready to change hideouts whenever the situation required. And sometimes their only salvation was provided by the monastic enclosure. "And here's something else that happened," Don Aldo recalled in that last interview. "I remember the case of the Finzi family, a father, mother and three-year-old daughter. They came from Belgium and were already in Assisi before September 8th and, therefore, had already been registered under their real names with the police. The mother and daughter had been staying with the Colettine Poor Clares. After September 8th the Germans began looking for them and the Bishop authorized the whole family to enter into the monastic enclosure, one of the strictest."

In the monasteries they succeeded in having two religious rites living side by side during that time. "It simply happened that in the quiet of the convents of Assisi," Don Aldo noted, "the Jews were absolutely free to assemble for prayer. We never did anything to disturb their religious expression. With great emotion I still recall that October 8, 1943 when the Jewish refugees of different nationalities gathered in secret in a room of the Monastery of San Quirico, which we had decorated for the occasion, to celebrate the solemnity of Yom Kippur. It was clearly understood that there were no refugees, only our brothers and sisters, and that we were united in a single prayer: that this tragedy would end soon."

Everything proceeded without particular difficulty until the afternoon of May 15, 1944 when Don Aldo was arrested at the entrance to his apartment on Via San Francesco. Asking to go back upstairs to get his breviary, he managed just in time to save a Jewish family who were waiting for him in the house. He was tried in Perugia and sent to a school that was being used as a holding place for the detainees. Through the influence of the Bishop Vianello[4], he was released by an agreement with the prefect. He would be free if he agreed to go to another State, namely, the Vatican. There he worked with Bishop Montini[5] in the Secretariat of State. So he was unable to see the allies enter Assisi on June 17th, but he knew that everything had gone smoothly.

"We Jews who were given refuge in Assisi will never forget what was done for our salvation. In a persecution that annihilated six million Jews, in Assisi not one of us was touched," said Emilio Viterbi in relating his dramatic experience as a refugee and expressing the gratitude of all those who had been saved.

---

4   Archbishop Mario Vianello of Perugia, Ordinary from March 1943 until his death in September 1955.

5   Bishop Giovanni Battista Montini, the future Pope Paul VI, who served as "*sostituto*" Secretary of State in charge of "ordinary affairs." On November 1, 1954 he was named Archbishop of Milan and was made a bishop on December 12th of the same year.

After the war Don Aldo returned to Assisi where he continued his priestly ministry, faithful to his role of obstinate defender of the values of freedom and tolerance. One had only to go and find him in his little bookstore a short distance away from the Piazza del Comune and see how his eyes would light up with the pride he felt for the whole community and hear from his lips the tales of those dark years marked by concrete actions of solidarity and hospitality. His whole priestly life was inspired and guided by a passage from the Sermon on the Mount: "Blessed are the peacemakers, for they shall be called children of God."

Paolo Mirti

Don Aldo, what were your first contacts with Jewish culture?

I knew the world of Judaism from my studies in Biblical theology. I studied Hebrew when I was taking theological courses in Rome. I remember reading the history of Israel by Abbot Ricciotti, a student of Lagrange at the Biblical Institute of Jerusalem, and I was impressed. It was a very precise story written brilliantly from an historical point of view. My relationship with Judaism stopped there for a long time. There were no Jews living in Assisi, in fact, until those events that followed that fateful September 8th.

Tell us about your childhood and your youth in Assisi.

I was born in 1914 into a lowly family. My father, Antonio, followed in a long generational line of rope-makers. He made ropes of coconut fiber imported from India to make the *fiscoli*, a type of coconut basket in which they placed olives for pressing. I remember walking for kilometers with him to go to the mill where he would repair the *fiscoli* that

---

1   Interview by Paolo Mirti a week before Don Aldo's death, in L'Avvenire on 25 January 2007. Translated by Nancy Celaschi, OSF. Used with permission.

had burst. He worked all day long and for supper we ate *bruschetta*. My mother was a homemaker, but she also took in sewing for the farm families. She was known for her ladies' corsets, and in payment she would receive chickens or eggs. My mother wrote very well, and I recall how the girls, with husbands or boyfriends at the front, would go to her to write letters to their loved ones. My parents made many sacrifices to allow me to study. I attended the classical secondary school and then the pontifical major seminary where I received my degree in theology in 1934.

How were your relations with the Fascist regime?

Well, I was of that Catholic cultural bent that did not accept the Fascist principles. I was an active member of Catholic Action, which was historically a thorn in the side of the Fascist ideology. Besides, relations between the Church hierarchy and Mussolini's government were not exactly idyllic. Already in 1931 Pius XI published a very strong encyclical against the Fascist regime on the topic of education of youth that threatened to undermine the treaty that had been signed recently between the State and the Church.[2] When Hitler arrived, in order not to be obliged to receive him, Pius XI went to Castelgandolfo. So, you see, I was a son of that climate and that culture.

Were you pressured or intimidated by the regime?

I suffered the effects of the dictatorship most of all in the

---

2   The Lateran Treaty was signed on February 11, 1929.

academic world. In the institute where I was teaching, the principal wrote a letter to the commissioner of education asking how he should behave towards me since I was unpopular with the regime. The commissioner proved to be an extraordinarily honest person who always protected me. Only later did I realize that I was being observed. At the 12 o'clock Mass that I celebrated every Sunday as a canon of the cathedral, certain persons came purposely to listen to what I had to say and to report it to those who sent them.

Don Aldo, what happened in Assisi after September 8, 1943?

Refugees in all kinds of conditions flowed into the city, people who had lost everything in the bombardments. And so in the diocesan office, at the request of Bishop Nicolini, whose closest collaborator I was, we created a Committee of Assistance with many volunteers involved. We had to take care of all the needs of those poor people for housing, food, and clothing.

When did the Committee start seeking refuge for the Jews?

It was a Thursday towards the end of September 1943. The Bishop called me aside. "I received instructions from the Secretariat of State," he said. "They asked me to offer aid and assistance to those being persecuted, particularly the Jews. This is Pope Pius XII's desire." He urged me to the greatest caution. No one must know anything. From that day onward, Assisi's convents and religious communities began to hide hundreds of Jews.

What made many Jews choose Assisi?

I think first of all they hoped that in some way Assisi would be spared. Then too, there was a practical, logistical matter. At a certain point the number of refugees in Assisi reached about 6,000 people, an amount that equaled the city's population. Under those conditions it was relatively easy to conceal the presence of two or three hundred Jews. And then, too, Assisi was accustomed to housing outsiders.

How did the underground organization work?

Everything was under the direction of Bishop Nicolini, who was the real person behind the work of saving the Jews. The headquarters was the monastery of the Poor Clares of San Quirico. There and in the guest house of the Holy Cross Monastery of the German sisters, the first to arrive were housed until we managed to get new identity cards for them that gave them the right to obtain ration cards. With these false documents, some of them were able to live undisturbed in a hotel or in apartments with families. It was often necessary to hide objects too: sacred books, family mementos, liturgical objects. We hid them in the basement of the Bishop's house, in recesses that the Bishop and I then proceeded to wall up. Bishop Nicolini personally laid the bricks while I held the candle. When the walls needed to be broken into, I undertook that work.

How did you get the false documents?

The identity cards were printed by two typesetters from Assisi, Trento and Luigi Brizi, in their shop in Piazza Santa Chiara, where they had a small pedal-powered printing press. Then too, we had a very careful female collaborator in the municipal office, an employee from Padua, who provided us with the real forms for the identity card. The most complicated part was the stamps. I recall that I sent Trento Brizi to a friend of his in Foligno with 50 lire and my bicycle to have them made. The false identity cards of course had to refer to cities in the south that had already been liberated, such as Lecce or Bari, so it would be impossible for the Germans to check into them. And sometimes it happened that women, whose documents stated that they were from the Bari, spoke with a purely northern dialect. In these cases too, we were ready with a perfect explanation: "Well, you know, I've been living in the north since I was a little girl."

What tricks did you use to avoid detection?

Well, it was impossible to be too careful, and we had to suspect everyone and everything. I remember that one day a German visitor came to the monastery of the German sisters of Holy Cross. We were afraid that he might have been a spy charged with infiltrating our organization. As soon as the mysterious guest went out, I remember that we entered his room to search it. To our surprise we discovered that he had left Germany to escape Hitler's regime.

Then, too, we always had to be ready to move refugees

when and if the situation demanded it. I recall how once there were rumors that the Nazis would conduct a sweep-search. The Jewish family of Giulio Corinaldi from Milan was staying at an inn with false documents, and did not feel safe. So I thought about moving them to Valfabbrica, in the mountains between Assisi and Gubbio, where I knew a parish priest who I was certain would help me. I no sooner arrived in Valfabbrica and found the town was swarming with German soldiers and Fascists checking out the area. I realized it just in time to turn around.

Were you also compelled to authorize the Jews to enter into the monastic enclosure in certain cases to ensure their protection?

That also happened. I remember the case of the Finzi family, a father, mother and three-year-old daughter. They came from Belgium and were already in Assisi before September 8th and, therefore, had already been registered under their real names with the police. The mother and daughter had been staying with the Colettine Poor Clares. After September 8th the Germans began looking for them and the Bishop authorized the whole family to enter into the monastic enclosure, one of the strictest. Little Brigitte would run around among the sisters. If the poor husband wanted to go out into the garden for some fresh air, he had to put a veil on his head to blend in with the sisters. A few weeks after the liberation little Maria Enrico Finzi was born in the monastery.

But how could two religious rites live under the same roof?

We managed quite well. After the liberation an English newspaper even wrote that the Jews were able to have a synagogue in the crypt of the monastery founded by St. Francis. That's not exactly what happened. In the stillness of the convents of Assisi, the Jews were completely free to assemble for prayer. We never did anything to disturb their religious expression. With great emotion I still recall October 8, 1943 when the Jewish refugees of different nationalities gathered in secret in a room of the Monastery of San Quirico, which we had decorated for the occasion, to celebrate the solemnity of Yom Kippur. It was clearly understood that there were no refugees, only our brothers and sisters, and that we were united in a single prayer—that this tragedy would end soon.

In a scene from the film, The Assisi Underground, a Catholic rite is celebrated in the refugees' presence.

For the love of God, this scene is pure fiction. And it's not the only one. I'll say it again. None of us ever betrayed the faith of our persecuted brothers and sisters.

"TOUGH" AND "RIGHTEOUS"[1]

Carlo Cianetti

"Tough" and "Righteous!" These two adjectives not only describe the personality of Don Aldo Brunacci, but they also sum up his life. And even though they are nicknames, they seem to augment his person.

"Tough," because Don Aldo belonged to a "tough" family, the Brunaccis, who throughout Assisi were known for their solid and determined temperament, but also for their longevity. His brother Lillo and his Aunt Lella were both well into their nineties when they died.

"Righteous," because the name of Don Aldo is found in the "Garden of the Righteous" in Jerusalem, together with those of Giorgio Perlasca, Marcella Gitelli, Odoardo Focherini, Giovanni Palatucci. All of these were heroic people who risked their own lives to save the Jews from the Nazi Fascist persecution.

Don Aldo was almost 93 when he died. He left behind an aura of religious and cultural activity, a journey of ideals and moral rectitude.

He was a young priest when in 1943-44 he helped Bishop

---

1   *È morto Don Aldo, "Il Duro" nel "Viale dei Giusti,"* by Carlo Cianetti in PRIMO MAGGIO, translated by Nancy Celaschi, OSF. Used with permission.

Placido Nicolini to find refuge for Jews in Assisi. He set up an association whose membership included two Communist printers (Luigi and Trento Brizi), a Franciscan friar (Rufino Niccacci), the mayor of Assisi (Arnaldo Fortini) and perhaps even the German Colonel (Valentin Müller) who, as head of the military hospital, was in charge of the whole city of Assisi. It was a philanthropic association that hid and protected scores of Jews. The result was, to the delight of all, that no one in Assisi was arrested or deported to the Nazi extermination camps.

With Don Aldo's death Assisi loses an important moral reference point—a man who struggled for freedom even under the threat of death, a man with a moral backbone, a righteous one, a tough one!

IN MEMORY OF DON ALDO BRUNACCI[1]

Claudio Ricci

Don Aldo Brunacci was an important example for Assisi, a reference point for all of us. More than words, his works spoke for him, especially his acts of charity. He was a man who, throughout his earthly journey, always worked for the good of the community and for others.

He gave us his charism, his enthusiasm, his complete self without stinting right to the end. He was a shining example of an ecclesial vocation, a model priest, a refined writer, a man committed to youth, and very supportive of the Italian Catholic Scouts.

Wonderful were the efforts he made, together with the late Bishop Placido Nicolini, the Franciscan family, and all the citizens for the "salvation of the Jews" in 1943-44 when Assisi became a "hospital city" that was able to welcome everyone, alleviate suffering— both physical and moral— and offer a "splendid example to the whole of humankind." For this reason, Don Aldo was recognized by the State of Israel as "Righteous among the Nations," and by the President of the Italian Republic as "Knight of the Grand

---

[1]   Claudio Ricci, Mayor of Assisi, in Subasio, periodical of the Accademia Properziana, anno XV, n. 1, 31 March, 2007. Translated by Nancy Celaschi, OSF. Used with permission.

Cross."

I recall the great joy with which he participated in the ceremony in Rome on 25 April 2004, when the city of Assisi was given the "Gold Medal for Civil Merit." However, more than these titles, we will preserve the memory of a person with a "great heart filled with love" who broadened the horizons of hope in so many other hearts.

Last Christmas Don Aldo, who felt that his earthly journey was coming to an end, in faith requested the sacrament of the Anointing of the Sick. It was for him the last Christmas that he lived in the hope of having accomplished everything possible in this earthly life and ready to follow the "pole star" into heavenly life. A star—his teaching—that we will look to forever!

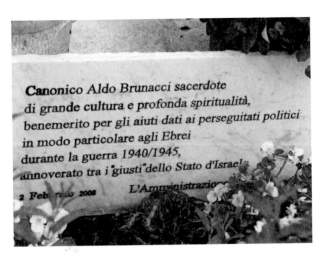

Plaque placed on Don Aldo's grave by the city of Assisi reads: Canon Aldo Brunacci, priest of great culture and profound spirituality, well known for help given to the politically persecuted, especially to the Jews during the war 1940/1945, counted among the "Just" of the State of Israel.

ASSISI WILL NOT FORGET BROTHER ALDO[1]

Marina Rosati

"Chosen associate, apostle of Christ," "exemplary priest and refined writer," are words taken from the homily of Bishop Domenico Sorrentino and the eulogy of the Mayor of Assisi, Claudio Ricci, which described Don Aldo Brunacci, a priest of the diocese of Assisi who died Friday morning, 2 February 2007, and whose funeral was celebrated yesterday in the Cathedral of San Rufino.

The cathedral, crammed with people, all of Assisi under the ensign of the commune, had come to pay him final homage. It was a heartfelt homage, one due him for a long life spent in behalf of others from his activity during World War II when he saved hundreds of Jews persecuted by the Nazi Fascist regime to the creation of his pride and joy, Casa Papa Giovanni, where thousands of pilgrims have come and lived in simple Franciscan style. His relatives, friends, those who lived with him, representatives of all the political parties, institutions, and major local associations—the whole city gathered in San Rufino where Don Aldo served as Prior and its most knowledgeable expert.

In recalling the most important aspects of his recent

---

1   By Marina Rosati in Corriere dell' Umbria, 4 February 2007. Translated by Nancy Celaschi, OSF. Used with permission.

acquaintance with Don Aldo, Bishop Sorrentino could not fail to emphasize "the man of faith that he was. When I came to know him, I was impressed by the pride with which he conducted the activity at Casa Papa Giovanni and the bookstore which, as he wrote in his last will and testament, must continue its work. He portrayed in a passionate manner a Christianity marked by a congeniality that was contagious."

And, as the Mayor said, Don Aldo "spoke with his deeds and his many acts of charity. We will preserve the memory of a person with a great heart filled with love who broadened the horizons of hope in so many other hearts."

Obviously moved, the hundreds of persons who filled the cathedral were even prouder of their fellow citizen when a representative of the Jewish community from Perugia read and translated an Aramaic prayer dedicated to Don Aldo.

The coffin left the cathedral on the shoulders of other diocesan priests who carried it to the hearse which processed through the city. First it stopped in the Piazza del Comune where the city officials and the people of Assisi rendered him homage, and then stopped in front of his much loved Casa Papa Giovanni.

When the cortege reached the cemetery of Assisi, his body was laid to rest in "Mother Earth," in the simplicity and humility that marked Don Aldo's life. Now Assisi's challenge is to remember what Don Aldo did for the Jews and others, so that this part of Assisi's heritage can be handed on to future generations.

LET US NOT FORGET
OUR BROTHER, DON ALDO[1]

Michael Chiariello

Don Aldo Brunacci, Prior of the Cathedral of San Rufino, Assisi died in the early morning of February 2, 2007. He was best known to the St. Bonaventure University community as a 2002 recipient of an honorary degree for his heroic work to save hundreds of Jews during World War II. And thousands of pilgrims remember him as their host at the Casa Papa Giovanni. In the summer of 2002, Don Aldo gathered several pilgrims from St. Bonaventure University, including Sr. Margaret Carney, and myself and asked why we didn't bring more students to Assisi to study their Franciscan tradition. I recalled that conversation as I led the very first class of students in the Franciscan Heritage Program to Assisi that very morning.

Several weeks earlier, Judy and I had gone to Assisi to pay our respects to Don Aldo. We found him bed-ridden and weak. I informed him that I had finally brought students to Perugia and Assisi. He seemed to have a twinkle in his eye when he complimented my "progress" in learning Italian. When I asked how he was feeling, he smiled and simply replied, "Ninety-three years, ninety-three years." That

---

[1]   By Professor Michael Chiariello, St. Bonaventure University, NY, February 12, 2007. Used with permission.

was to be my last encounter with Don Aldo before his appointment with Sister Death.

I did not know that as I entered Casa Papa Giovanni on a spectacularly sunny morning a few weeks later. After the students and I had hiked up from San Damiano to Santa Chiara and then across town to a lunch appointment just a few doors from Don Aldo's home, I left the group to call on him, and to inquire whether he would be strong enough to grace my class with a brief visit. Instead I walked into his wake. "E' morto!" announced Rita, his devoted assistant, as she led me to his casket in the tiny chapel by the front door. And so he was. To his distinctive bearing of strength and gentleness, now was added peace.

The funeral was the very next day at his beloved San Rufino. It was a remarkably local affair for a man I had always considered a global citizen, and whose walls boasted tributes from world leaders and celebrities. Now the church was packed with family and Assisi neighbors, including the local boy and girl scout troop that he had once led, wearing their uniforms and holding high their hand-made wolf and bear banners. Of course, there was a tribute from the President of Italy read by Mayor Claudio Ricci, and a stirring tribute from Assisi Bishop, Domenico Sorrentino. The Bishop recalled Don Aldo as a man with a "passionate and contagious" Christianity, who "spoke with his works and many acts of charity" and "whose big heart of love broadened the horizons of hope for so many."

But surely the most dramatic moment in the service occurred when a diminutive bearded man, Professor

Gustavo Reichenbach, donned a Jewish yarmulke and began to recite the mourner's Kaddish in Aramaic. A chemistry professor at the University of Perugia, he represented the remnants of the Jewish community there, which includes some who survived because of Don Aldo's courage.

The next day the *Corriere dell'Umbria* reported that this tribute made the Assisians even more proud of their citizenship, which seems amazing enough in the birthplace of Francis and Clare. But I understood. My moment of pride had come just before when Bishop Sorrentino described Don Aldo's special appreciation for his honorary degree from "L'Universita' di San Bonaventura a New York."

Grave of Don Aldo Brunacci (†2007), cemetery of Assisi

The newspaper's headline read, "Assisi non dimentichera' fratello Aldo" to which I'm proud to add, "Amen, St. Bonaventure University, let us not forget our brother Don Aldo."

Don Aldo Brunacci, 1914 - 2007

ANOINTING DON ALDO BRUNACCI, RIGHTEOUS GENTILE[1]

Murray Bodo

You're sitting up waiting for
the anointing, telling me

War horses pound through the walls
menacing hooves above you

Knights rear back in their saddles
their swords slice the stagnant air

Some say it's the morphine which
Can't be true in 1209 you say

Bocce balls bang hard outside
Hooves thrash in a mad frenzy

You scream mutely as in dreams
bracing yourself for the blow

And no one hears or answers
though the fresco teems with life

---

1   By Franciscan Poet, Murray Bodo, from *Autumn Train*, Tau Publishing, 2015.

For hours the hooves delay
pounding your head to pieces

You wonder why you see knights
not Nazis and Fascists in

Assisi in war time or
Jews you hid from the evil

I answer, "They're now in your
soul's peace where there are no walls"

I minister healing oil
Hooves drop, slide off your forehead

Your eyes close, you dream good dreams

DON ALDO BRUNACCI (1914-2007)[1]

Murray Bodo

Pigeons sleep on the railings
of windows opposite mine.

Echoes pulsate from the stones
where I last saw Don Aldo,

a frail 92, his cane
gently tapping away from me

toward the Piazza Comune
at the end of Via San Paolo.

I watched him walking, it seemed,
forever, and the piazza – like

the Jewish refugees he sheltered
and saved from harm – was

receding from his determined will.
I see him walking still,

his short shuffle out of step
among friends and passersby.

---

[1]   By Franciscan Poet, Murray Bodo, from *Autumn Train*, Tau Publishing, 2015.

A PRAYER FOR WISDOM AND STRENGTH[1]

Don Aldo Brunacci

"May the Lord give you peace!"
(St. Francis of Assisi)

Lord, merciful, almighty, Creator of heaven and Earth,
we praise You for Your glory
and thank You for Your love and protection.
We are gathered here today in Your name.
You have entrusted us
with the gift of leadership of a great Nation.
Give us the wisdom and the strength
we need to fulfill our mission according to Your will.
Help us never to betray our mission
but to do Your will
in respect and obedience to our own conscience.
Give us the gift of discernment
never to falter in our decision-making.
Lord God,
You have treated our Nation with great generosity.
Help us to treat others
with kindness, generosity, and justice.
Give us peace of mind and heart,

---

1   Editors' note: Don Aldo Brunacci offered this prayer in the House of Representatives, Washington, DC, 24 March 2004.

that peace which comes from You.
Grant peace to our families,
to our Nation,
and to the whole world.

a cura di:

OPERA
CASA
PAPA GIOVANNI
ASSISI

MUSEO della MEMORIA
ASSISI 1943-1944

Orario mostra

Da Novembre a Febbraio:
10.30-13.00
e 14.00-17.00

Marzo, Aprile, Maggio, Settembre, Ottobre:
10.00-13.00
e 14.30-18.00

Giugno, Luglio, Agosto:
10.00-13.00
e 14.30-19.00

Per non dimenticare
Mostra sugli ebrei salvati in Assisi nel periodo delle persecuzioni naziste

ASSISI - PALAZZO VALLEMANI
PINACOTECA COMUNALE

A MUSEUM OF MEMORY

An Exhibition in Assisi

It was in a spirit of Franciscan hospitality that about three hundred Jewish people's lives were saved in Assisi during World War II. And today there is an exhibition to memorialize this slice of Assisi's history.

As soon as one enters the first exhibition gallery at the Palace Vallemani on the Via San Francesco housing the "Museum of Memory, 1943-1944 Assisi," one can immediately sense the historical period.

The idea to have this exhibition was conceived by Marina Rosati, in collaboration with Casa Papa Giovanni and with the former Bishop of Assisi, Sergio Goretti. English translations of texts were done by Annabella Donà. The exhibition includes unpublished documents, photos, awards, essays, and articles about that historical period and the various protagonists who gave of their own lives to help save the Jewish refugees.

The exhibition displays the work of Don Aldo Brunacci, the priest Bishop Nicolini chose to direct the operation of hiding the Jews; Bishop Giuseppe Placido Nicolini, who guided the underground organization that spontaneously had arisen in Assisi; Friar Rufino Niccacci, guardian of the Franciscan sanctuary of San Damiano; Arnaldo Fortini, the mayor of Assisi; the German commander, Colonel Valentin

Müller; Friar Michael Todde, and others who did their best to preserve the lives of many Jewish people otherwise destined for deportation to death camps.

One important section of the exhibition is dedicated to Luigi and Trento Brizi who printed false identity cards for the Jews. Besides viewing the antique printing machine used to produce the false identity cards at the museum's entrance, the exhibition displays the actual printing equipment used by the Brizis.

The exhibition, in both Italian and English, winds it way through four galleries that include some writings, a documentary film featuring interviews with some of the protagonists given before their deaths, relating what was done by people in Assisi to preserve the lives of so many Jews. The exhibition is open daily at the Municipal Gallery of Assisi.